SHAYNE
WARD

MY STORY

SHAYNE
WARD

MY STORY

To my mum and my family, who always believed.
And to my fans, who made my story happen.
Thank you always.

Copyright © Shayne Ward 2006

The right of Shayne Ward to be identified as the author of this work has been
asserted by him in accordance with the Copyright, Designs and Patents Act 1988.

First published in hardback in Great Britain in 2006 by
Orion Books
an imprint of the Orion Publishing Group Ltd
Orion House, 5 Upper St Martin's Lane,
London WC2H 9EA

10 9 8 7 6 5 4 3 2 1

A CIP catalogue record for this book is available
from the British Library.

ISBN-13: 978 0 75288 564 3 (Hardback)
ISBN-13: 978 0 75288 634 3 (Export Trade Paperback)
ISBN-10: 0 75288 564 2 (Hardback)
ISBN-10: 0 75288 634 7 (Export Trade Paperback)

Printed and bound in Great Britain by Butler and Tanner

The Orion Publishing Group's policy is to use papers that are natural,
renewable and recyclable and made from wood grown in sustainable forests.
The logging and manufacturing processes are expected to conform to the
environmental regulations of the country of origin.

Every effort has been made to fulfil requirements with regard to reproducing
copyright material. The author and publisher will be glad to rectify any omissions
at the earliest opportunity.

www.orionbooks.co.uk

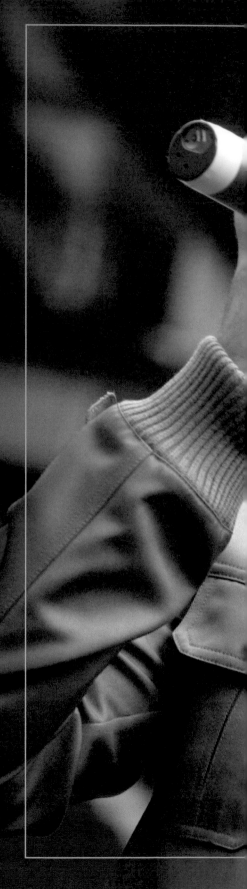

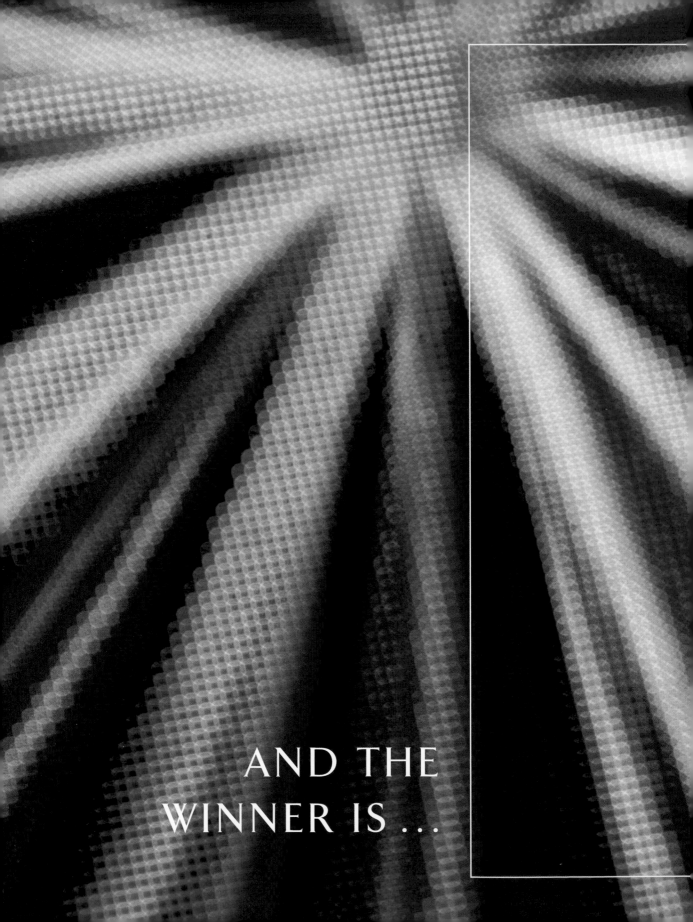

AND THE
WINNER IS ...

THE ATMOSPHERE
WAS SO TENSE
YOU COULD HAVE
CUT IT WITH A
KNIFE, AND EVEN
IN THE STUDIO
THE AUDIENCE'S
HYSTERIA SEEMED
TO HAVE TURNED
TO FEAR

I was waiting backstage with Andy and Journey South. My hands were sweaty and my heart was thumping with nerves because I knew at any minute we would be called on stage to hear who would be crowned the winner. At no point did I ever think it would be me – I was convinced Andy would win and I think the rest of the contestants believed that as well – but the buzz of the show took over and I could hear the audience cheering and going wild. I was terrified. All I could think was, this is what I've waited my whole life for, but I knew it could go one of two ways.

Waiting in the wings with the other guys was tense to say the least; the atmosphere between us had changed somehow and become really intense. We were all so nervous by that point that the odd reassuring glance was pretty much all we could manage. I was trying to focus on keeping it together when we walked on stage and deal with the possibility that in just a few moments my dreams could be shattered. As I walked out into the heat of the studio lights my head was spinning and all I could make out was Louis walking towards me. I felt weirdly numb, and for the first time everything around me became a blur. I didn't seem to be able to take anything in, and even when Louis stood beside me I couldn't relax.

It had been quite a long night and we had all sung three songs each and watched each other perform on a small television in the group dressing room. Although we were competing, everyone was really supportive of each other; being under that kind of pressure was hard for all of us to deal with, so it was nice to have the other lads around for reassurance. Deep down we all knew how much each of us wanted to win, but none of us allowed that to get in the way of helping one another through the evening. I don't think any of us had ever felt pressure like that before, and with your nerves up in the air it was hard to perform to our best ability. Every time one of us sang we would text in a vote for each other – I guess it was our way of showing support.

Louis looked every bit as nervous as I was and we both just stared straight ahead. Simon stood in the middle with Journey South, being the ever cool and calm but nervous under it all Mr Cowell, and Sharon was holding hands with Andy. The atmosphere was so tense you could have cut it with a knife, and even in the studio the audience's hysteria seemed to have turned to fear. It was possibly the most nerve-racking moment of my life, and waiting for the announcement seemed like the longest few minutes ever. Journey South were the first to be knocked out – I think they were surprised because every week their support and votes had been very high, but it was a close final and one of us

had to go first, and at that point I was just relieved it wasn't me. It also confirmed my worst fears, though, because I'd always thought Andy would win as he was such a strong favourite with the other contestants. After Journey South went, I thought my time was up as it was one down and another one to go. I was praying it wouldn't be me. My hands were scrunched into little balls by my side, I was so stressed. Then Kate Thornton stopped for an ad break – I couldn't believe it – just as I thought she was going to announce the winner she said we would find out after the break; it was so awful and she kind of looked like she was enjoying it. She had a big grin on her face as we all stood there petrified – looking back I suppose it added to the tension.

Finally the moment had come and I could feel a lump in my throat as though I was about to cry. I was frozen with fear as Kate slowly said, 'And the winner is ...' There was a horrible, long pause. I couldn't bring myself to look at my family and friends in the audience; I couldn't look at anyone, because I knew if I did I'd lose it. I just stared into space, waiting for the name to be called. By that point I was thinking, please just put us out of our misery! Some sort of suspense music was playing to make the whole thing more dramatic and I thought everyone must be able to hear my heart pounding as I stood there secretly praying. I could hear the odd person scream out my name and then Kate said them, the words that would change my life for ever ...

1

24 HOURS
TO LIVE

Ever since I was a child I wanted to make my mum proud and give her the happiness she and my three brothers, Mark, Martin and Michael, and my three sisters, Lisa, Emma and Leona, deserve. We haven't had it easy. My mum brought all seven of us up on her own, so she had her hands pretty much full and got very little time for herself. I was born in Hattersley in Cheshire, but like everything in our lives, nothing went smoothly, and when I was born on 16 October 1984, two minutes after my twin sister Emma, the doctors gave me just twenty-four hours to live. Although I was bigger than Emma, weighing 5lb 6oz to Emma's 4lb 12oz, she was the healthy one. My mum always said she was small but strong and I was big but poorly. I was two months premature and my lungs hadn't fully developed, which meant I had to be put in an incubator and left to try and breathe on my own. Emma was put in an incubator too, but more because she was small than because anything was wrong with her. It was touch and go whether I would survive and Mum spent every night by the incubator praying I would get through another day. Because my lungs and chest had caved in, the doctors weren't very hopeful that I would make it and Mum told me she was terrified of losing me. She couldn't bear to hold Emma without me, but she was told that it was unlikely I would survive given how under-developed my lungs were. But as each day went by, I defied the odds and my condition improved, then after about two months my mum took me home. I was fine and as I got stronger my breathing improved and I've luckily never suffered from any side effects due to my early start in life.

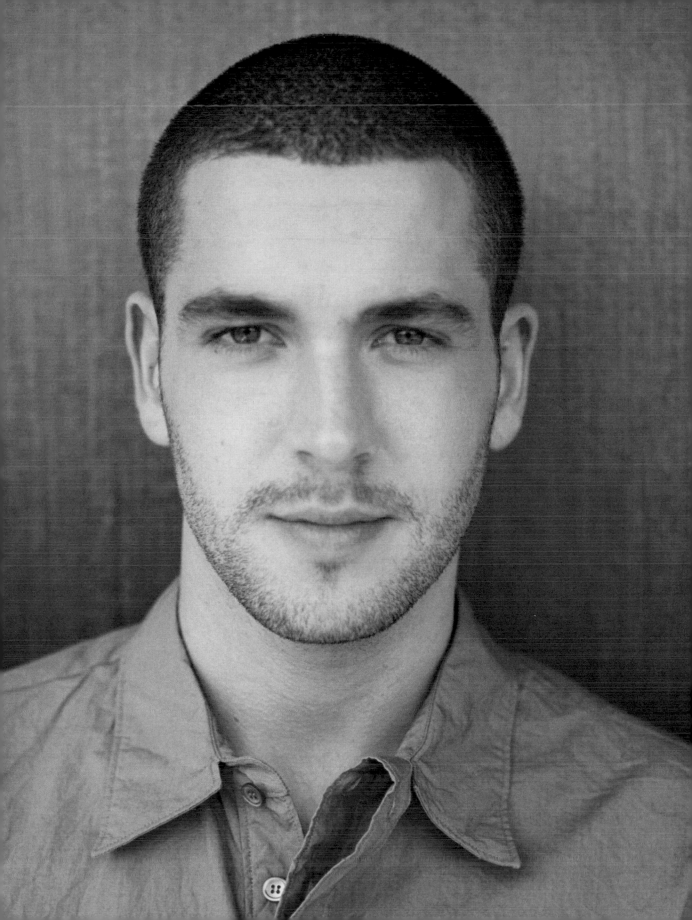

WE WERE KIDS AND WE HADN'T COVERED OUR TRACKS VERY WELL

We lived in a four-bedroom detached council house then, when my dad was still around and before Mum and Dad began running pubs. I remember it being massive. It had a big bathroom upstairs and a downstairs loo, a big kitchen and quite a big garden with a ginnel (that's northern for walkway) under my mum and dad's bedroom, through to the garden. Emma and I have always shared a room, and although I'm close to all my brothers and sisters, I think we have a special bond, though I'm glad we don't have that weird thing where we feel what each other feels – that would be a very strange sensation. There are occasions when I say something and she says she was just thinking the same thing, but to be honest that's about it and all seven of us are very close.

Emma was so messy that she would take up more than half the room with all her stuff; her clothes were always lying around everywhere. She used to say it was pay-back time for the nine months when I took up all the space in our mum's tummy! We were as thick as thieves and would get up to all sorts of naughty things when Mum wasn't looking. We even had our own language, which no one else could understand, and it used to drive my mum mad.

Once, when the house was being decorated and Mum was busy helping upstairs, we'd been quiet for quite a while, which usually meant we were up to something, so Mum came to look for us. She found us in the downstairs loo, where I had taken a pair of scissors to Emma's hair and cut all of the back off – she was literally bald – and she had cut off my long black curly hair, which was my mum's pride and joy. Mum went crazy, and I mean crazy; she couldn't believe that we had been so stupid, but even when she was telling us off we wouldn't admit that we had done it. We'd shoved all the hair down the toilet and even stuck the scissors down there, too, trying to hide the evidence, but we were kids and we hadn't covered our tracks very well – all the hair was sticking to the inside of the bowl. Mum took us straight to the hairdresser's and we both had to have our heads shaved because there was no other option. Emma was mortified because we looked a bit like twin boys. She was so upset with the way she looked that she refused to go to nursery.

Emma and I both had favourite blankets, mine was blue and hers was pink and they went everywhere with us. But when they needed to be washed I hated it and would kick up a right fuss. When my mum eventually got her way, I'd sit in front of the washing machine and watch it go round and round until the cycle finished. I think I must have been a really patient child because the wash lasted a fairly long time. Emma didn't have quite the same patience and wasn't bothered, but me and my blanket were inseparable.

It's funny looking back at all the things Emma and I did together – now we don't even live in the same city. I find that hard and often think about the good times we had together when I lived at home. We didn't have a care in the world at that age. Mum and Dad were still together and Emma and I would get up to as much mischief as possible. We had a terrible habit of writing on the walls.

Mum would get so angry, but it never stopped us. We thought we were being very clever because we wrote in code, so only Emma and I knew what it meant – at least for a while, before Mum worked it out. We would write back to front, so you could only read it when you put a mirror up against it. It's fair to say Mum wasn't impressed and we often used to get sent to our room.

There's about eight years between me and my eldest brother, then there's Martin, who's six years older, Michael who's five years older and Lisa who is just two years older than me and Emma. Then after us there's our little sister Leona. We were always playing games together, and I think Mum found the extra help from Martin, Mark and Michael was useful. I don't think they changed any nappies when we were babies, but they would always look out for us and take us places when we were too young to go on our own.

The house in Hattersley was always busy with people coming and going, and with so many of us we would inevitably find something to keep ourselves amused. While Emma and I were close, we would always join in with the others and we weren't inseparable; it was only when we started school that we used to stick together like glue. The house had loads of steps – you would walk in and steps would go one way to a landing, then the other way to a balcony. I must have been about six when we used to climb down blankets from the upstairs balcony to the ground. Martin, Michael, Mark

SHAYNE WARD: MY STORY

and Lisa would put blankets underneath the drop, which was pretty steep – if I'd have fallen I would have really hurt myself – and then I used to carefully work my way down. Mum went mad when she found us, but it didn't stop me having another go. I was always up for some fun and a challenge, and we were used to thinking up new things to keep us occupied. With seven of us at home and money so tight, we couldn't always be out and games like these would help pass the time.

We also used to play hide and seek, but the last laugh was always on me. One time, my brother Martin suggested hiding in a suitcase, which at the time I thought was a pretty good hiding place, so I jumped in, he zipped it up and then pushed it down the stairs. Looking back, it's quite funny – I was so little and so keen to join in that I fell for their tricks every time. One memory that really stands out is the dressing-up competitions we used to have. We would lay out socks, shorts, jumpers, hats and tops all in a pile on the bed and race to see who was the fastest to put them on and take them off again. We loved that game; it was basic but it kept us amused and we were quite competitive.

All of us can sing except my sister Leona, who gets very frustrated about it. She used to shout, 'Why am I the only one who can't do it?' which we all found quite funny. She would try and sing along with us, but she just didn't have the ear for it, and when we sang along to the radio or a tape she always found it hard to hit the right notes.

One of my sisters' favourite films is called *Streets of Fire*. It's about a female singer who's kidnapped by some bikers and is eventually saved by a guy who she falls in love with. She performs two songs, one at the start of the film and another at the end, and we all loved them because they're two great tunes. When we were young, Emma, Leona and I would stand on the couch, press play and wait for the song to start so we could copy her. We used the video remote control as a mike and had a great time singing the song over and over again.

Christmas is probably my favourite time of year, mainly because I love Christmas music. Being winter it would get dark early, and Emma, Lisa and I would go outside to check if the stars were out. We had a little ritual where on clear nights we would rush out into the back garden, stand on two crates and sing 'Silent Night' – we used to do that every time there was a clear sky. I don't think anyone was listening, but it didn't matter to us, we just loved doing it, and used to imagine our crate was a stage and we were performing to a big crowd of people. Christmas was a special time for me because we were all together – at least in the early years. Presents weren't a big thing, it was more about being a family and spending time with each other. We didn't have the money for fancy presents, but none of us went without and we always had a magical day.

Even in my early childhood, music meant a lot to me and we would spend loads of time listening to my parents' records; those tunes had a big influence on my life. I think if you're around music and people that enjoy it you soon learn to express feelings that way and become creative. I was always quite shy except when I used to sing, then I'd lose myself in the music.

My mum and dad would always have music blaring when they got ready to go out. We used to listen to lots of Elvis, country because my mum loves Patsy Cline, Connie Francis, rock 'n' roll and Irish music because of our family being Irish. I have never lived there, but Mum and Dad were born there and moved to the UK when they were young, which is why my mum doesn't have much of an Irish accent. Two songs that really stand out in my memory, though, and which were played over and over, were 'We're Going To Barbados' – the Venga Boys did a version of it called 'We're Going To Ibiza', but the original was about Barbados – and Queen's 'I Want To Break Free'. Every time I hear those songs they bring back happy memories of when I was younger. All of us would sing along using pretend microphones and the smell of hairspray was so strong it would choke you – and that was just from my dad's hair! He had a big, crazy barnet like Kevin Keegan's – that was the fashion at the time, I suppose, and that's what my dad had.

Mum and Dad were known as Mena and Martin, and they were the karaoke king and queen of our area. Mum would dance while she was on stage and shake her hips at a hundred miles an hour, and I'm not exaggerating. Her specialities were 'The Locomotion', 'Will You Still Love Me Tomorrow' by the Shirelles and Patsy Cline's 'Crazy'. When she sang karaoke I was so proud of her. We didn't have a karaoke machine at home to practise on, we just made do with pretend microphones and sang along to the music on the stereo. Although I have to say I'm thinking of buying her one now – she'd love it!

There were a couple of pubs in Hattersley, one called the Underwood and another the Flat Cap, where my parents would go regularly to sing karaoke, and the landlords and punters knew they would always put on a show. They had a presence about them, and people knew that if Martin and Mena were there they were guaranteed to have a good night. I think it was because they were such a fun couple and used to be the life and soul of the party.

Sometimes, as a special treat, I would be invited down to the pub to watch them sing, and I loved that – I felt so proud watching Mum and Dad perform and seeing everyone having such a good time. I was desperate to have a go myself because I loved singing, but I

was a bit young, and besides, I would have been too nervous at that age to sing in front of all those people. I can remember my dad buying everyone drinks – that's what it was like when I was a kid and my parents were together: we would have fun and be a family. I would sit at a table with my orange juice and look around thinking that everyone loved my mum and dad, and feeling fantastic.

If we weren't allowed to go to the pub we would often wait up for them to come back from their night out. One of my older brothers would look after us while they were out and would let us stay up until they got back, probably because they remembered doing the same thing when they were younger. We would all rush to the door when we heard the keys go in the lock because we knew that if Dad had been drinking we would get some money. I don't have many memories of my dad, but I do remember him being generous with his cash when he'd been out for a drink, and that he would often take us down to the chip shop. It was a real treat to get a takeaway and we'd be allowed to get as much food as we wanted, then take it back and eat it in the living room while he fell asleep. In the morning he'd say, 'Where's all my money?' And we'd say, 'Don't you remember, Dad, you took us down the chippy last night.'

We moved from Hattersley when I was about six to a pub called the New Inn in Clayton, where Mum and Dad became landlady and landlord. We lived there for a couple of years before moving to another pub called the Folkstone. It was great fun living in pubs; we used to love it as kids because it was a bit of a novelty and quite social, with lots of different people coming in each day. Mum and Dad seemed to enjoy it, too, and it meant they could sing karaoke whenever they wanted. On weekend mornings I can remember waking up and hearing Mum and Dad cleaning up downstairs, so Emma and I would tiptoe down and hide under the tables. The idea was to jump out and give them a fright, but I would always end up popping my head out and offering to dust or clear some glasses. I was quite helpful like that as a child and wherever I could I'd lend a hand, but I'd be silly, too, and Emma and I in particular would mess about thinking we were being cool. We'd pour lemonade and Coke together in a glass and pretend we were drinking cider or beer to try and trick Dad, but he'd just come along and say, 'I hope you two aren't drinking beer?' knowing full well what we were up to.

Having a jukebox had to be the best part of living in a pub, and before opening time we'd be allowed to go and play whatever we wanted for free. All of us loved music so much that it was playing all the time and we'd take it in turns to choose the tunes we wanted. I don't think it ever got a rest while we were about, and I'm surprised we didn't wear it out. We'd dance and sing along while my mum polished the bar, and if I think really hard I can imagine us all there, one big, happy family.

Sometimes we would even get to play the odd free game of pool, and that's how I met my mate Shaun. He was one of a group of lads who would pop into the pub and come and play a game with me. I thought I was the business when I lived in the pub, and having unlimited access to a pool table and jukebox did wonders for my street cred. I used to pretend I knew a trick to make all the balls come down without having to pay. I'd tell people to look away and then knock my elbow on the side of the table and all the balls would appear. In fact I had the key, but it worked and everyone thought it was a pretty good trick and would ask me to do it over and over again. Shaun and I lost contact for a while after that, but weirdly we met again when I moved to Clayton, and we're still close friends now.

My mum and dad split up when I was ten and Dad moved away; I was still young at the time and didn't really understand what was going on. I knew he'd moved away, so I wasn't completely in the dark, but it was a strange time and a lot changed in our lives. For one we had to move out of the pub, and that was hard because we'd had such fun times there and none of us wanted to go, but with just my mum it wasn't possible for us to stay as she couldn't run the pub on her own. I knew there were problems between my parents because I would hear them rowing some evenings, but at that age you don't question it. It was hard to see my mum hurting, though. She used to cry quite a lot, and all of a sudden there was a lot of pressure on her, not only financially but emotionally, to look after us all. She tried to put on a brave face and hold us all together, but I could see that things were getting to her and that she was down.

I think any parent would find it hard to suddenly be single and left with seven children. I think we understood how difficult it was for Mum, and for that reason we were pretty controllable and didn't give her a hard time. I was only ten, but when you're a kid you're pretty intuitive and can sense when things aren't right, also having older brothers and a sister who would mention things to me here and there helped. From them I gathered that things just weren't working out between my parents and that one day my mum had finally stood up to my dad. They loved each other, but she just reached a point where she couldn't cope with his aggressive behaviour and so she ended it and told him to leave. Dad needed to be responsible for his own actions and to be prepared for the consequences, and those were Mum asking him to leave. The bottom line is that he was no good with drink and my mum had reached breaking point.

When Dad moved away there was no question of us going with him – there was no way we were going to leave our mum. We did have the choice, but I could never have left Mum's side. It didn't have anything to do with my age; even if I'd been older there's no way I would have gone with him. I didn't see Dad for a year after that, and that was probably the hardest part, because up until then he'd always been there and I was used to having two parents around. My dad was always about carrying barrels in the pub, cleaning up or watching TV, then suddenly he was gone, and that was really hard to get my head round.

Dad moved to Liverpool, and although I knew that there had been rows and that every marriage ends for a reason, I wasn't aware of what it was. I just thought they had fallen out of love. When we did go and visit him in Liverpool, Emma, Leona, Lisa and I went up by coach. My brothers didn't visit him; they were older and could make their own decisions. When we arrived we'd sit watching home video tapes of us that we had made, playing them over and over again and reminiscing about when we'd all been together. The videos were of us getting ready for a fancy dress party, or when Mum was pregnant with our Lisa, and I think they made Dad upset because he never wanted the marriage to end, even though he knew it had to.

I've tried my best to see the positives in my parents splitting up, and I do think it's made me stronger as a person. It's definitely brought the rest of us closer together. Mum has become our life, and that goes for every single one of us. At the end of the day you only have one mum and we love her unconditionally. My parents' separation has made us a stronger family, without any doubt. We had to be strong for Mum, and although she has quite a few brothers and sisters, we were always there for her, too. There isn't much that hasn't been thrown at us and yet we've still survived. Don't get me wrong, we aren't saints and my brothers and sisters all argue, but that's just normal. Generally we get on pretty well and, as siblings go, we're very close.

I think I have an old head on my shoulders for a twenty-two-year-old. After my dad moved away I could have gone either way, down a good path or a bad one. It would have been easy to fall into the trap of hanging round the streets of Manchester, robbing cars, drinking, being violent or damaging property. That's what happens in so many places to so many people, but I didn't want that; it seemed like the easy option. Besides, my mum was never going to let me take the wrong route, even if I'd wanted to. She loves us all too much to see us throw our lives

way like that, we are her babies and she wouldn't let us fall in with a bad crowd if she could possibly help it. Michael used to love being on the streets, though, and he could easily have chosen a really bad path at one stage if he'd wanted to, but he didn't. He realised there was more to life than hanging about the streets and eventually he stopped, much to my mum's relief. I thank my mum for keeping us on the straight and narrow – she never let us stay off school, and if we did, which wasn't often, she never knew about it. She was desperate for us to get some sort of an education; if she hadn't things could have been very different.

Once Dad had gone we moved into another council house on Fifth Avenue in Clayton. It was fairly small, but it was all we needed because by that point it was just Mum, me, Emma, Leona, Lisa and Michael. My other brothers had all moved out, got jobs and were more or less looking after themselves. They were only a stone's throw away from us and when Michael turned sixteen he moved in with Martin (the ladies' man) in a flat nearby. They both worked in security and used to give Mum some of their wages to help us out.

My eldest brother Mark became a butcher and still works in Ashton. He has two kids of his own with his ex-girlfriend, and now lives with his new girlfriend in a flat in Ashton.

Clayton is quite a nice place compared to some of its surrounding areas. People make out that you walk out your door and get shot but it's really not that bad, that's just over-exaggerated newspaper talk. I always felt very safe there and I lived there for almost ten years. Besides it can't be that bad as there are two of us from Clayton who've made good, me and Ricky Hatton – a boxer who's doing really well for himself. He went to Hattersley High, which is the same school my brothers went to, and they knew each other quite well.

I have many happy memories of my years in Clayton. I loved living in Fifth Avenue. We had the house right at the end of the road and I made so many friends it was kind of like a youth club. Although it was really hard for Mum bringing us all up on her own, and money was very tight, Mark's wages helped out, and as each of us got older we were able to go out, get a job and bring home some money. Somehow we survived; I think mainly because Mum is a fighter. We always managed to scrape by, get clothed, fed and washed, and a lot of my clothes were hand-me-downs from my brothers, but I didn't mind and it was a good way of saving money. When you have so little cash even the smallest amount makes you feel rich – if I found 50p I'd think I was loaded. We never really went without as such. Mum had an amazing way of disguising our financial worries, and always protected us in that way. Obviously we know now that things were very tight, but at the time she never showed it. She wouldn't burden us with the strain she was under and would give us everything she had to ensure we were happy. I'm sure that on many occasions she would go without just for

Mum held down whatever jobs she could to make ends meet. Mainly she cleaned local pubs or worked in factories. She once worked in a biscuit factory, which was great because she used to come home with loads of biscuits for us to eat – I liked that job.

Even when she was working so hard to bring in the money she still managed to wash and iron our clothes and school uniforms, and she'd always have our tea ready when we got home. Mum would do everything to make sure we had what we wanted, and every birthday we'd get great presents. I remember telling her that I didn't want clothes with designer names like the other kids at school. I didn't want her to think that because she saw other kids wearing Adidas and Nike she had to buy me the same. I told her I didn't care and that I'd wear whatever she bought me, which I did, but she still tried, and once she even bought me a black Man United shirt. I've always loved Manchester United and I couldn't believe it, I was so happy. It was the best present I've ever had and it meant so much. I can remember turning round to her, with tears in my eyes, saying, 'Mum, you really didn't have to do that.'

We did go without in some ways, though. We didn't have holidays because we couldn't afford them and it was very rare for any of us to go on a school trip. Mum always said that if she let one of us go she had to let us all go, and she just couldn't afford that. Blackpool was one of the only places we went to, and even then we only went for a day trip. It was Michael's school trip to Blackpool beach and we all tagged along – me, Mum, Emma, Lisa and Leona. We went on the coach with the rest of the pupils and teachers and I can remember being so excited. As soon as we got there we started playing in the sand while Michael was with the rest of his class swimming in the sea. We didn't have any buckets and spades to build sandcastles with, so Mum being Mum went off in search of some. You'd have thought it would have been an easy mission, but it wasn't, she was gone for ages, searching everywhere, and when she finally came back we were over the moon. It was never going to be a happy ending, though, and just as we were filling our first bucket with sand, the schoolteacher in charge blew her whistle and announced that it was time to leave. Mum was so upset and we felt upset for her because she'd spent all that time looking for a bucket and spade for us to have only two minutes enjoying them before we got back on the coach.

We'd often go for picnics and think of them as a holiday because it was something different and fun for us all to do. We'd have to find alternative ways to take a break, but when you've never had something you don't tend to miss it, and that was with the case with holidays for us. We had each other, that was enough.

2
SCHOOL DAYS
AND FIRST KISSES

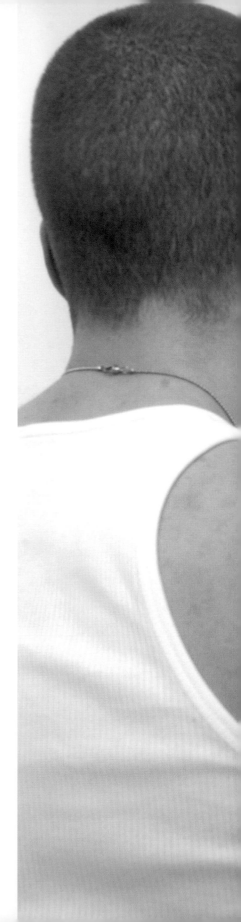

My memories really start from the age of nine or ten when we'd just moved to Manchester. I think I joined Ravensbury School in year 5 and Emma and I used to hang around together all the time; we wouldn't leave each other's sides. We would get the 171 bus to school together every morning and come back together in the afternoon. Emma and I would even spend break times together, which wasn't the best idea socially because we didn't really make any friends. Mum would always be around when we got back from school, either cleaning, doing the washing or shouting at one of us to stop messing about. She's the tidiest person ever, and even with so many kids running about she was in total control of the house. If she walks into a room and it looks dirty she has to get the hoover out because she absolutely hates a mess. She always says she likes a clean space, so we tried not to leave our dirty clothes on the floor.

In the mornings I was a nightmare. I hated getting dressed into my uniform. I don't know why but I really didn't like it. To avoid the inevitable I would very often try to get away with falling asleep in my uniform just so I wouldn't have to get dressed the following morning. Mum wasn't impressed with that at all and would tell me off. I thought it was a genius idea, but she wasn't buying it. I'd go to bed and she would shout, 'Shayne, you are not going to bed in your uniform!' so I would have to change. Mum would make us our breakfast and then go back to bed after we'd left. She would pack us a lunch box and leave two or three quid on the side for us to buy our bus tickets. They were called clipper cards – instead of us paying money each day we'd get a clipper for the week and the bus driver would clip it off day

I KNEW SCHOOL WAS
IMPORTANT AND
ALTHOUGH I FOUND
IT HARD, I DID TRY
MY BEST

OF TONY;
IT WAS
A REAL
HONOUR
AND I
WORKED
SO HARD
LEARNING
MY LINES
AND
PRACTISIN
SCENES
AT HOME

by day so we didn't have to carry loads of cash about. Any money we had left over would buy some crisps or sweets on the way to the bus stop. We would save as much money as possible for sweets. One time I remember saying, no more sweets; I'm going to save for a guitar – it's fair to say I never saved enough to buy one.

It was at about this time that I had my first girlfriend; she was called Toni and lived in the same avenue as we did. She had ginger hair and we went out for quite a while. It wasn't a serious relationship – we were only ten after all – it was just a little friendship and it felt cool to call her my girlfriend! We didn't go to the same school, but we saw each other most nights. She bought me a chain with half a heart on it and she wore the other half, which is quite sweet when you think about it. My first kiss was with Toni and it wasn't the most romantic setting. There were a few of us: me, Toni, her friend, my mate Shane and his brother Paul were all together and while nobody was looking we literally ducked into a shaded area and kissed. We were both hopeless at it and we couldn't get the hang of it at all but I have very fond memories of those innocent days, everything so new.

Secondary school was a totally different ball game. I really began to find my feet at St Gregory's, which was a Catholic school, and I made loads of friends. It was like any other school, with its different groups of people. The popular crowd had their group and the not-so-cool people had theirs and we were somewhere in the middle, which is why I think we fitted in quite well. If we walked past the cool crowd they'd say, 'All right, Shayne,' whereas other people would get a heap of abuse thrown at them. There were five of us that hung around together – Phillip Berry, Warren Williams, Graham Murdoch, Thomas Finnegan, Anthony McKewin and me – we were inseparable and would play football every spare minute we had.

Most of my mates wagged school, bunking off lessons wherever possible, and I did too, once or twice. I suppose most kids try it because they want to experience what it's like and I wanted to be like my mates. We wouldn't do anything bad while we were skiving, though, we'd just go down to the tennis courts nearby and play football, or occasionally we'd go to Graham's house and he would make us really disgusting sandwiches.

Even at that age I knew it was important for me to get an education, and although I found school hard, I did try my best. My favourite teacher was Mr Savage. One year he compered a talent show we did, and as I love singing I got involved. In fact, I still have the tape of my performance somewhere. I sang the Westlife song 'Swear It Again', and at the end Mr Savage said to me, 'I should manage you.' Everyone laughed at the time, but I'd love to know what he thinks now. I was always very shy at school, but when it came to things like getting up on stage and performing in front of people, my love of music seemed to take over and I lost all my inhibitions, much to my brothers' and sisters' amusement. Often the parts I'd play would mean I had to dress up, and I have been known to wear tights on occasion in some of the Victorian plays we put on – my brothers and sisters thought that was hilarious. The talent show was probably the first time I performed properly in front of an audience, and I enjoyed it so much I knew it was what I wanted to do with my life – all I needed was the opportunity, but that was the hard bit.

While I was at St Gregory's it merged with two other schools – St Vincent de Paul's and St Alban's – and became St Peter's, but there were massive teething problems at first, with lots of kids getting bullied. Fortunately I wasn't one of them, but I did see it happen, especially to swotty kids in the younger years – the ones who were top of the class – who got kicked and had their bags stolen by gangs of bullies. My brothers are very protective of me and if anything like that had happened they would have stepped in for sure. It took a little while, but slowly things started to calm down and people began to mix and get on better as we all realised we were at the same school and should get on with it. The best part about the school merger was that one of the other schools brought a Performing Arts class with them and in year 10, when you can choose what subjects you want to take, that was my first choice, along with Art and PE. Ms Kennedy was my Performing Arts teacher and

was fantastic, definitely one of my favourites. She brought my confidence out and made me believe in myself. I have alot to thank her for. I played loads of different parts while I was at school and even managed to get the lead role in Westside Story, which meant that as well as acting I got to sing too; it was only after that that I got into acting in a big way. I loved playing the part of Tony it was a real honour and I worked so hard learning my lines and practising scenes at home. The more I practised the better I got and the more confident I became on stage. It's weird because when you enjoy something like that it's never a chore and it was something I did willingly in my spare time.

During *X Factor* I went back to St Gregory's to perform. It was the first time I'd ever travelled in a helicopter and it was just before the final, when all the finalists visited their home towns to drum up support. The school didn't seem to have changed much from when I was there, except that there were pictures of me hanging everywhere. It's funny how when you leave school you think all the teachers are old when they're really not. When I went back they didn't look any different. I was with Louis and we flew from London to Manchester and then had a police escort from the heliport to the school. It was such a buzz and I felt really special.

It was an amazing experience going in the helicopter – I've never done anything like that before and if I'm perfectly honest I didn't think I ever would again as it probably cost a fortune. It was great to see that Louis seemed to be enjoying it just as much as I was; he's probably been in a helicopter more times than he can count, but he still seemed to have fun. Louis is great; he has no airs and graces and is totally down-to-earth. I think if my feet even slightly left the ground he'd be there pinning them back down. It's as if Louis has a little map in his head and knows exactly where me and my career are going. I want to fulfil his dream as much as my own, and am working my hardest to do just that.

Mrs Connely was my RE teacher and I got on really well with her, too – I think she was the only teacher to ever get any homework back from me. My family is Catholic and when my parents were still together we'd go to mass every Sunday morning, which I really enjoyed. We'd all go together, my brothers, sisters and Mum, and it was great fun, but once my dad went that kind of stopped, which was a shame. I still went to mass with the school, though. We had a choice of going to mass or joining school assembly in the hall and I always went to mass. I do believe in God and it meant something to me to go to church.

I was a really good lad when I was at school and didn't get myself into any trouble. The only thing I'm gutted about when I look back is that I didn't do better. I know for a fact that if I'd listened and paid more attention in lessons then I would have done well, but I was always too busy having a good time. Warren sat next to me in class and I always thought his answers seemed more intelligent than mine, which I think knocked my confidence a bit. I would look at Warren's answer and it would be

exactly the same as mine, just worded differently, and I'd be convinced that his sounded more intelligent. Warren always helped me out, though. I was pretty useless at doing my homework; in fact, it was pretty much non-existent except for RE. I could never get my head round coming home from school to sit down and do more work. I found subjects like Maths really hard, and instead of trying I just wouldn't bother, which would frustrate my mum no end. She was always trying to get me to do better but I'm not sure what the problem was: I just wasn't focused on work. My mind was on other things … like girls.

I was about fifteen or sixteen when I started properly fancying the ladies. I was going through puberty at the time and my hormones were rampant as my body was changing. I was well chuffed when my moustache started growing. I think I was about fifteen at the time and at school we'd all compare our growth, with some boys saying proudly, 'I've got hair coming out of my chin,' and others saying 'Oh, I haven't got any yet.' It's a funny time growing up, and with all those changes going on I was often distracted from knuckling down to homework, and with all my sisters around it could be hard to concentrate, too – I think that's probably why my homework never got done.

My school reports were always quite average. They'd say things like 'Shayne could do better'. The only subjects I did really well in were Performing Arts, RE and PE. I used to love PE, and not just because of the sport. We would spy on the girls all the time, sneaking a peek through their changing-room door when it was open and screaming at the half-dressed girls. It was brilliant. I'm sure that's the sort of thing all boys do when they're that age, but if the girls caught us we'd be in big trouble. We did all sorts of sports at school, but my favourite was football. I'm a massive Man U supporter, although I've never been lucky enough to go to a game and have only ever watched them play from the couch. I've always wanted to go to a match, though.

and it's definitely on my to-do list. At school I played in the football team for a while and was actually quite good, so maybe if my luck changes I'll turn my hand to that instead.

PE was always the last lesson before lunch and we'd spend ages making sure our hair looked good before going out for lunch break. With our hair wet and our shirt buttons slightly undone, showing off our growing pecks, we thought we looked pretty cool.

I wasn't a swot but I did what I needed to do to get by. My biggest problem was thinking I wasn't intelligent enough, but I can't have been as stupid as I thought because I passed all my GCSEs in the end. They weren't the best results, but they weren't that bad either. I got mainly Bs and Cs, but I got an A1 in Performing Arts, as well as A grades in PE and RE. Maths was the one I did least well in, and although I've always struggled with it, I know that had I worked harder I could have done better. I got my results at the end of the summer holidays and Mum was really proud of me – I think she was pleased that all her nagging had paid off.

Over the years my friendship with Warren and the other lads cooled and we haven't kept in touch, which is a real shame. I don't have any of their numbers to try and contact them, but I'd love to meet up with them again. I think as you grow older people often grow apart and lose contact, and nowadays my close friends are the guys that lived near my house in Fifth Avenue in Clayton – Gareth Cartledge, Ben Reiley, Dan McCann, who we call desperate Dan, and Gracey, who was Ben's stepbrother and lived next door to another friend, Tina.

The first time I met Gareth was when we'd just moved into our house on Fifth Avenue. I was walking up the road when I saw him playing football with a couple of neighbours and I sat on the wall and watched. It wasn't long before Gareth asked me my name and if I wanted to play a game with them, and that was it. From then on we were best mates. If I stood at my back door and looked across I could see Gareth's house, that's how close we lived, so it was easy for us to play together every day. I met Ben after Gareth. I'd seen him riding his bike in the avenue a few times and he stood out because he never wore a top. I got to know Ben through Gareth and we'd all play football together.

Dan was the last recruit to our gang, and I met him at a youth club called Crossley's. They ran a music programme called Music Stuff, and that's how I met Dan. The music programme was the only reason I went to Crossley's – it was a great opportunity for kids to record material and be around like-minded people. I enjoyed it because I love anything to do with music, and it was the only chance I had to use that sort of equipment. I went once a week after school, and the days in between couldn't pass quickly enough, but when I was there the time literally flew by. It wasn't a cool place to hang out, it was just a place where people with a real passion for music could go, and as far as I was concerned it really opened the door for me. It probably kept a lot kids off the streets, too, because it gave us the chance to make a hobby out of something we loved doing.

Dan became part of our crowd quite quickly after that. Gareth, Ben and I used to play computer games a lot as we got older, but when Ben started going out with a girl called Tina we'd all go round to her house instead. Tina's dad was called Mick and he was great because he'd let us have little parties. We were so happy doing that, playing football in the avenue and going to each other's houses, that I don't remember trying to blag my way into clubs. I had older brothers to take me places like that. My brother Mark sometimes took me to a pub called the Royal Oak where all the ladies loved him, and I used to feel really big tagging along with him. I don't know what it was with my brothers, but the women used to fall over themselves for them and going out with them was so much fun. I think being that bit younger made the trips seem really cool; my brothers certainly seemed to handle themselves well, and while I'd be all shy and quiet at the table the ladies would literally hang off them. I'd never expect the girls to pay any attention to me because they were far more interested in my brothers, and if a girl did ever look my way I'd think they were looking at Mark, Michael or Martin.

As I got older I became more independent and started going to the pub with my mates and spending lots of time out and about. I was beginning to have a mind of my own and started making my own decisions, although I was still quite heavily influenced by my brothers. When I was sixteen I decided to have my first tattoo done. I think any child with older brothers aspires to be like them – I know I did – so when I was legally allowed to get one done I went straight down to the tattoo parlour. The first one, a Chinese symbol on my right shoulder, is a very small S for Shayne – I think I wanted to check I liked them before having anything too drastic done. I had it done in Wales when I went away with some mates, and although I did ask my mum's permission beforehand, I was still a

bit nervous about having it done. After the first one it was easy and I've gone on to have several more. I have a leprechaun on my right arm, which I had done in Clayton, and a shamrock etched onto my left arm saying 'Luck of the Irish' underneath, which I had done in Newquay. Every year me and the lads would go to Newquay for a few days to play football and we'd have a great time. The last tattoo I had done was a fairly big tribal one, and the guy who did it claims he did David Beckham's angel.

Apart from my tattoos I wasn't particularly rebellious – I don't smoke, only have a drink on the odd occasion and have never touched drugs because I'm too scared of them. I think my not drinking much is down to the first time I got drunk, which wasn't a nice feeling at all. I was in Ashton on a night out with my eldest brother Mark when I started to feel ill, so Mark put me in a taxi and gave the driver my address to take me home. When I finally got home Lisa came to the door and said, 'God, you're a mess.' I was falling into the bushes and everything, and when I eventually managed to get through the front door I fell asleep by the loo. Lisa called my mum to tell her I was drunk and that she couldn't get me into bed, but Mum just shouted up the stairs, 'Shayne, are you comfy?' And I said, 'Yes,' so she said, 'All right, good night.' She was just winding up our Lisa and eventually she came up and helped lift me into bed. I felt pretty rough the next day, let me tell you.

I've always taken pride in the way I look and never went through phases of dying my hair crazy colours or wearing bizarre clothes. My hair was black and curly and there was nothing I could do with it, no matter how I tried. I'd put gel on it but it had a mind of its own, so I could never let it grow really long and always had the same kind of cut: short back and sides. I was almost the opposite of most kids my age, who all seemed to be going through dodgy phases. I had all sorts of funny rituals and insisted on my clothes being neatly ironed – I couldn't bear it if

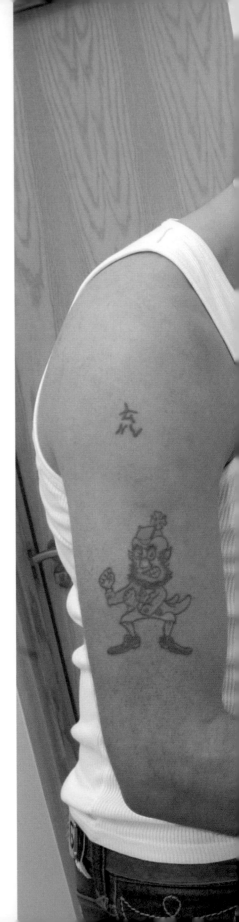

I WAS STILL QUITE HEAVILY INFLUENCED BY MY BROTHERS

something had a crease in it. My sisters used to wind me up about that all the time, as if I suffered from an obsessive compulsive disorder. I just liked to take care of myself, but I'll admit I had a few weird habits. Don't ever give me a piece of Blu-Tack to play with because I can't leave it alone. I roll it up, then throw it and then find it again – I'm a nightmare with the stuff. My sisters laugh at me because I'm the same with bread – I'll get a bit, crush it down and roll it like Blu-Tack.

Me and my friends used to have sleepovers at each other's houses a lot when we were younger – usually at Gareth's – and we got up to all sorts of naughty things. Nothing bad as in with the police, just naughty schoolboy things. It was usually me, Gareth, Paul and Shaun, and we used to play jokes on each other. When we were about seventeen we had a sleepover, and for some reason Shaun brought his comfort pillow with him – I'm not quite sure why he still had one at that age, but he did (bless him). While he was asleep we put toothpaste all over his hand and then tickled him a bit so his hand went up into his hair. It was only in the morning that he realised what had happened, by which time the toothpaste was everywhere, especially in his hair, and it's not easy stuff to get out. He wasn't the only one who got tricked, though. Paul had a thing about wanting to be Cisco, the singer, so while he was asleep we poured talcum powder into his hair so it went white blond. When he came downstairs the next morning he didn't realise what we'd done until everyone cracked up, which only made it funnier. It was brilliant.

We had so many good times together, but these days I hardly ever get to speak to them. I do phone occasionally, but I haven't managed to see them for months. It's hard with them being in Manchester and me in London and I do miss them all.

3

DREAMS
ON HOLD

I think the only thing I regret is not continuing with my education. If I'd focused I reckon I could have done quite well, and I think my love of the performing arts would have pushed me to knuckle down and go to college. At the time, though, I had other priorities, such as wanting to help my mum. I needed to get a job so that I could start bringing some money in, and that meant leaving school straight after my GCSEs. It was just me, Emma and Leona living at home then and I was desperate to start contributing and paying my way; if I could earn money I could pay her rent and that would help out a lot. I have always been fairly independent, so no matter what anyone said I'd have done the same, and I think that even if I hadn't won *X Factor* and wasn't where I am today I wouldn't think I'd made the wrong decision because it did help Mum a lot. I also think that having a few years' work under my belt has been a good thing because it helped me learn how to focus and concentrate my mind on things, something I was never very good at at school – it definitely helped me on the show. Even if I had decided to carry on studying, I'd still have had to get a part-time job to pay for it, and then I would have been knackered.

In the end it didn't take me long to find a job, and after a short interview with a local chocolate factory I started work there. The only problem was I really hated it. I was making chocolate – everything from chocolate bars to chocolate cakes – and it put me off chocolate for a good few weeks; only weeks, mind, not months. Believe it or not, being around so much chocolate was disgusting. I'd get a sponge cake, then I'd have to coat it in chocolate and then decorate it with Smarties. It was a bit like Willy Wonka's chocolate factory, which sounds like a dream job, but smelling chocolate every minute of the day eventually made me feel really sick. I think seeing how it's made put me off quite a bit as well, and every time I saw someone eating a chocolate bar I'd be like, 'Urgh!' Funnily enough, I didn't do that job for long.

After that I worked with my friend Gareth in a clothes factory that made airline jackets. I know I did some weird jobs, but they paid me money, so I was happy to do them. The clothing factory was where they used to film the scenes in Mike Baldwin's office in *Coronation Street* before it got burned down, so in a way I guess I was already mixing with the stars! Who would have thought then that I'd be where I am now.

I was still flitting from job to job, trying to find out what I enjoyed as much as anything, and

after the stints in factories I took a job in a printers. It was boring at first because I only used to get to put leaflets in folders and then into boxes, which was very tedious, but it wasn't long before I started to make the printing plates, which I really enjoyed. I used to get the metal plate, put the ink on top of it and then print it off.

I was about eighteen when the work at the printers dried up and I desperately needed to find another job. It was around this time that I started going out with Faye. I met her in a bar called Chambers in Ashton. Faye and I have been together for three years now, and despite what everyone says we are really happy.

The night I met her I was out with my brother Mark. We were standing on the balcony when she walked in and after I spotted her, I just turned to him and said how lovely she was and

that was it. I didn't mean anything by it, it was just a comment, but funnily enough she had said the same to one of her mates. Apparently she said to her friend, 'Have you seen that guy on the balcony?' So we obviously noticed each other straight away.

Mark and I were just leaving when I saw Faye again, so I made an excuse that I wanted to finish my drink before we left. I stood there finishing the dregs and was just about to bottle it when I heard someone shout, 'Oi!' It was Faye. That was her chat-up line! I turned round and said, 'Me?' And she was like, 'Yeah, come here.' I walked over to her table and sat down; her friend was sitting between us and we just chatted for a while. We didn't kiss or anything that night, we just had a nice chat and swapped numbers and that was it: the beginning of our relationship. I didn't go out that night to pull, and when I saw Faye I just thought it would be nice to have a friend who was a girl. Up until then all my friends had been blokes, and having a girl 'friend' was something I liked the idea of. But then about two days later I texted Faye, saying, 'So what do you say to going out, then?' And that was it, we started texting and talking and I wasn't thinking of her like a friend any more, I was really attracted to her.

Our first date was pretty special. I booked a room at the Diamond Lodge Hotel in Gorton in Manchester, which I think cost me about sixty quid at the time. I wanted to make the night really special so I asked my mum to help me organise something. We went shopping and bought white chocolate buttons and rose petals, which I scattered all over the bed, and I bought Faye's favourite wine as well as a bunch of roses and some candles. I even wrote her a poem telling her how the minute I set eyes on her I knew she was the one, and I had bought her a watch to remind her of that night. It was pretty romantic really. Once we'd finished decorating the room Mum said, 'Tell me how it went in the morning, son.'

Faye had been at work that day and I'd told her to meet me

"HEY LOVE, WHAT DO YOU THINK OF THESE?"

at the hotel, but I don't think for one minute she expected all that. I had dressed up in a suit and when she walked in I was sitting at the bar waiting for her. I asked her to wait in the bar for a few moments while I popped upstairs to light all the candles I'd placed around the bath. The wine was in an ice bucket and everything was prepared. I then went back downstairs to get her and took her back to the room. Her face was a picture; she really couldn't believe what I'd done. She was so shocked it was brilliant, and I can honestly say that that night went very well indeed! It was very romantic and I got the girl.

Luckily Faye's dad John gave me some temporary contract work with a company called TIS and I learned a lot there; ever since I've been quite handy around the house. I learned how to install cables for computer and telephone points, and soon I was working in schools and businesses installing cables every day. Faye's dad was just helping me out until I found something permanent as I was really unsure what I wanted to do and I kept asking everyone for advice. I can't think who it was, but someone said that I should try and get into the clothing industry, and, as I've always liked clothes: I thought why not? My first interview was with New Look in Manchester, because I thought they were opening a men's department, but when I got there I realised that wasn't the case at all. At the end of the interview they offered me the job and I took it. I could think of worse places to work than in a ladies' clothes store and at least it was a foot in the door. I was paid £500 a month and I got a discount off their clothes, which was great for Faye but not for me. I ended up working in the shoe department where I had a great time – it was a really sociable job because I got to meet loads of nice people. The worst part about it was having to pick all the shoes off the floor at the end of the day. People would leave them scattered everywhere and never put them back where they found them. What used to bug me the most was that just when I'd sorted a display someone would come over and reach

for the shoe right at the back, knocking the whole lot down. Once I found my feet – sorry, that was me trying to be funny – I started to keep a small bottle of air freshener in my trouser pocket. I couldn't believe the number of women with smelly feet! There was one woman who used to come in all the time and I could smell her before I saw her, but I'd be fully prepared with my air freshener and would spray it everywhere she'd been.

Working in a place like that you tend to see a lot of sights, good and bad. Women were always asking my opinion when they tried on shoes, which is quite normal, but one day a lady came in and I'll never forget her, as much as I try to. I was crouching down at the time, putting shoes on the bottom shelf of the gondola we used to carry the shoes, when I heard her say, 'Hey, love, what do you think of these?' I turned round to find

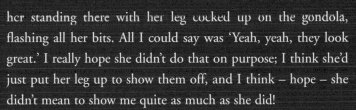

I WASN'T ANY GOOD WITH THE GIRLS

her standing there with her leg cocked up on the gondola, flashing all her bits. All I could say was 'Yeah, yeah, they look great.' I really hope she didn't do that on purpose; I think she'd just put her leg up to show them off, and I think – hope – she didn't mean to show me quite as much as she did!

One positive side of the job was that I got to see a lot of fit girls come in and out, so it was a great opportunity to eye up the totty. As I've said before, though, I wasn't any good with the girls and had no idea whether they were looking at me or not. Even when girls came up and spoke to me I thought they were just being polite; I had no idea they were being flirty. It wasn't until my mate Tracy got a job there that I found out girls were asking about me. Apparently they used to ask who the guy on shoes was. And Tracy would come and tell me who'd been asking. She loved winding me up about it and saying, 'I know you love it!' I guess I did a bit; it was quite flattering. All that female attention started not long before my first audition for *X Factor* in Manchester, and as I'm pretty shy around women half the time it went over my head – if I think a woman's attractive I can't look them in the eye. As time goes by I think I'm becoming more confident, but it's a real challenge for me and it's not something that comes easily.

It was great to earn some money and help Mum out financially; I felt like I was giving something back and doing something to help the whole family, but my first love was always music, and even when I was working, picking up the shoes and running around finding sizes, I would daydream about making a career out of it.

It was around the time i left school that I joined a band called Destiny, which consisted of me and two Tracys – Tracy Murphy and Tracy Lyle. They had always been a three-piece – before me they'd been joined by Tracy Lyle's sister Trisha – and were well known for singing karaoke in the local pubs and clubs. When Tricia left the girls needed another member, and Tricia had suggested my twin sister Emma. Coincidentally, a few days later Lisa, Emma and I went down to the Royal Oak pub to sing karaoke and the two Tracys were there talent spotting. Emma was up first and she got a great round of applause from the audience, then Lisa and I got up and did a duet, I think it was '(Everything I Do) I Do It For You'. We were just having a laugh but when we'd finished the Tracys thought, he's good, why don't we have a boy in the group? They came up to me and suggested it and I was really interested, so I went for an audition, got the gig and almost immediately started going round the working men's clubs singing karaoke. We didn't practice much – in fact, I can't remember us practising at all, because we all felt pretty confident about the way we sounded – and the reception we got in the clubs seemed to confirm that. We even had three agents who would get us gigs and take a cut of the money we made.

Singing in the band was only a weekend job, though, and I never gave up my full-time job because we didn't make enough money singing. At our first proper gig I have to admit I was terrified but as the evening went on I really began to enjoy

myself, and at that stage I didn't even realise we were going to get paid. I was there because I loved being in a band and I loved singing; the whole money thing didn't really bother me, it was second to the enjoyment. At the end of the evening Tracy passed me £30 and I said, 'Is this for me?' I tell you, being paid £30 to stand on stage doing something you love is a great feeling and I thought all my Christmases had come at once!

Destiny ended up being the most popular trio in the area and we were booked pretty much every weekend. We didn't get paid a lot but it was a labour of love more than anything else and we had a really good time doing it. I really miss the Tracys because we had a lot of fun and it was with them that I gained most of my experience and the ability to perform on stage without collapsing with fright.

We had so much fun together that even when we weren't playing we'd still meet up. One really hot day I was at Tracy's house, which is up near the cricket green, and we were playing music and being a little bit mischievous. The cricket club is just across the way and one of my friends called Robert came up with the idea of streaking for a laugh. He dared us all to do it and for some reason – I don't know why – I put my hand up and agreed. I dressed up in a thong (a male one I hasten to add) and a stupid wig and got ready to streak across the cricket pitch. Robert drove me to the top of the green, I took a deep breath and I ran out across the game. Thank goodness no one took any pictures, but all the players laughed their heads off and cheered.

My first audition for *X Factor* was while I was in Destiny. We sang our hearts out, but unfortunately we were turned down. I've since found out that the judges were considering asking me to go solo and putting me through, but it didn't happen, which is a shame. But it was an important step for me as the audition made me hungry to try again … so the following year I decided to go it alone.

4

WHAT DREAMS
ARE MADE OF

I didn't enter *X Factor* because I wanted to be famous; I entered it for my family. Originally my two sisters and Faye auditioned but didn't get through, and after that they were all on my back to audition – even my mum. They are the only reason I put myself forward as a solo artist after not getting through with Destiny. My first audition was in Manchester at the Lowry Hotel and I had to sing in front of the producers of the show – singing to the judges doesn't happen until you've got through the initial stages. I had missed the first audition because I was in Spain on holiday with Faye, a trip we'd saved up for, but luckily the day after we flew back there was an open audition, which I went to. It was being advertised all over Manchester and I think I was eating a pasty in my lunch break when I read about it and there was no way I was going to miss it. The audition was on one of my work days, so I needed to book time off. New Look were really great about letting me go, but eventually I had to hand in my notice in September when things became more time-consuming and I didn't want to mess them around; at that point I needed to concentrate on the final stages of the competition.

Although my confidence had been knocked from the first rejection I was determined that 2005 would be my year and I would give it my all. Finally, I was getting the chance to prove myself. I wanted to change my life, and although I enjoyed my job it I had to pursue my dream.

I sang in front of three people to start with – some of the producers and researchers of the show. It was a nerve-racking experience, but I figured I just had to give it my best shot; it's as time goes on and the pressure increases that it becomes scary. I can remember every stage of the auditions so well. It was such a lengthy process that you'd think I would have forgotten it all by now, but each part was so important to me that I think it will stick in my mind for ever. In the first audition I apologised if I was singing through my nose but I had hay fever and had just got off a plane from holiday – I really didn't want that to ruin my chances. I sang 'Sacrifice' by Elton John and a song called 'You Make Me Feel Brand New' by the Stylistics. I could see their faces staring back at me as I sang my heart out and at the end they asked me which one I thought I should sing in front of the judges. I said that I thought the Stylistics should be the first song and Elton John the second, but they disagreed, saying I should do it the other way round. They then passed me a piece of red card with 'Congratulations on getting through to the next round' on it. Once I had that card I walked back out into the waiting room, where people were still waiting to go in and sing. Everyone cheers when you come out with a

THERE WERE SOME CRAZY STORIES IN THE PRESS, BUT KATE IS A BUDDY

red letter but I don't think that part was filmed; I think they only pick up from the round with the judges.

Once I'd been given the thumbs-up by the researchers I had to get in a queue for the next bit, and by that point I was really nervous. I had to wait to be called in to see the judges, who were all sitting on chairs, and each time another person went in we would all move up a seat. My nails were bitten right down by the time it got to my turn. While I was waiting to go in I got chatting to a girl called Joanna Hindley, who ended up in Sharon's group at the boot camp stage. Bizarrely, Joanna and I knew each other vaguely because I had met her one night when I was singing with Destiny in a pub called Churchill's in the gay village in Manchester. She had asked me whether I was gay and I'd said, 'No.' And she'd said, 'Good, because you're gorgeous.' That kind of broke the ice a bit and after that she became good friends with my sister Lisa. Joanna had previously won a competition to duet with Westlife on their TV show *She's the One*, so I knew she was in with a good chance of getting through. She's so lovely and we tried to keep each other's minds off what was about to happen, but by this point I could see Kate Thornton wandering around and I was like, oh my God there's Kate! That made me even more nervous because seeing her made it all feel much more real. It's funny to think how nervous I was meeting her because now we are great mates. There were some crazy stories in the press about us getting together, but Kate is a buddy.

The queue was getting shorter and shorter and I knew that at any minute my name would be called. Suddenly the cameras were on me and it was my turn to go in – if they were trying to get a shot of me looking nervous it can't have been hard. The minute I opened the door Kate came over and asked me how I was feeling; she told me to go in and do my best and then wished me luck. It was my first time on camera and that alone was fairly nerve-racking. It was short and sweet, but I was so focused on what I was about to do that the conversation with

Kate seemed like nothing in comparison. As I walked through the doors, not knowing what to expect, I saw white arrows on the floor showing the way and a person directing me round the corner to where the judges were sitting. Then BOOM! There they were and I was standing right in front of all three judges, Louis Walsh, Sharon Osbourne and Simon Cowell, along with loads of other people – producers, directors, camera crew and the guy who would eventually become my co-manager with Louis, Ashley Tabor – and they were all watching me. After the shock wore off I just about managed to say, 'Hi, are you all right?' There was a brief conversation, which is a bit of a blur now, but I do remember Simon mentioning the leprechaun tattoo on my arm. They asked me why I had entered and I said it was because I thought I had as good a chance as anybody, and then they asked me what I was going to sing, so I told them 'Sacrifice' by Elton John, and Louis said, 'Right off you go!' That was it: I started singing.

I was trying so hard to concentrate on the song and not on where I was. I knew I was swaying from side to side and I had my eyes shut so I could focus, but I also knew I needed to make eye contact at some point during the song. When I finally did I could see Sharon smiling and Louis and Simon watching me closely which I kept telling myself was a good thing just so I could keep going! At the end of my first song I asked them if they wanted to hear the next one, 'You Make Me Feel Brand New' by the Stylistics. They all seemed to agree that it was a great song and they wanted to hear me sing it, but unfortunately my hay fever had other ideas and I wasn't able to hit the full falsetto – the really high note – which I was upset about, though the judges didn't seem to mind.

When I finished Simon said, 'Do you know what, Shayne, I like you. What I like about you is that you look real, you don't look stage school.' He then turned to Sharon and she said, 'Yes,' and then Louis said, 'It's a yes from me, too, you are through!' Little did he know he would end up being my mentor. Just before I left the room Simon said to me that he thought I seemed very calm and by that point I was. It was a really weird feeling and I said, 'Yes, I am and I don't know why.' On the way in I'd been incredibly nervous, but once I was there it was like the nerves just left my body. I shook the judges' hands and walked out. On the show you see me yelling at the top of my voice – it's like I'm crazy – and I walk over to Kate, hug her and lift her off the floor. It felt so amazing. The judges' comments after I'd left the audition room were quite something too – Simon said he really liked me and Louis thought I was good and could sing, while Sharon just said I had a beautiful face … and that was the start of me and Sharon.

One of the researchers had told my sister Lisa, who was waiting outside for me, that I had got through and she ran towards me in slow motion screaming, 'Shayne, come on!' And just at that moment Faye walked in after her A-level exam in Performing Arts and realised I had gone through – it was such an incredible feeling to have them there to celebrate with. When I went home and

announced that I had been put through, Mum was so happy and kept saying, 'I knew you could do it, I knew it.' I was still a long way away from winning, but the first hurdle was out of the way, and with each stage my confidence grew. I couldn't wait for the boot camp to start – once you've got that far you just want things to move rapidly so you can have a go at the next round.

The next phase was boot camp and there would be three groups of fifty people. The over twenty-fives, the groups and the under twenty-fives. My group, the under twenty-fives, had to meet at Finchley Art Depot in London, where we were split into two groups of twenty-five, and each group had to sing in front of the other. We all had to perform in front of Louis Walsh, Yvie Burnett the vocal coach and Faye Sawyer the stylist. I was one of the first to get up and sing on stage and I had a choice of songs. There was Christina Aguilera's 'Beautiful', 'Unchained Melody', a Bee Gees number called 'To Love Somebody' or George

Michael's 'Careless Whisper'. Like nearly everyone else, I chose to sing 'Unchained Melody', but everyone seemed to start it in a different key and I began panicking, thinking, which key shall I choose? When it was my turn I walked on and said, 'Hi, I'm Shayne Ward and I'm going to be singing "Unchained Melody".' I was so nervous that I started in the wrong key – it was way too high – but as the song began building up and the highest part got closer I managed to hit the note. I couldn't believe I'd done it, it was such a relief. I managed the falsetto and brought it all the way back down and it worked. Just as I was finishing I looked out into the audience and at the back there was a guy with braids who was laughing at me; it was so off-putting and made me feel so self-conscious because he was clearly taking the mick out of my voice. I managed to finish off, though, and Louis said thank you before I walked off stage. Louis later made a point of saying that he loved the falsetto part of my song – the bit I'd been worried about.

That was when the wait really began and I started praying I'd go through to the next round. People said how great I was after my performance and that I would definitely get through, but I wasn't so sure, for all I knew they could be saying that to everyone. What I didn't know was that while I was on stage Ben Shepherd had been asking the other people auditioning who they thought would go through, and apparently nearly everyone said me. I was only told that later on and it gave me

goose bumps. Ben told me they were saying, 'The guy in the red with the cap is definitely going through.' The best bit about watching the other people perform was seeing the bloke who had laughed at me go up on stage – he was crap, one of the worst voices I've ever heard, and needless to say he didn't get through.

When everyone had finished performing we had to wait before we were split again. Our names were called out and we were placed on different sides of the stage – I knew one side was going home and thankfully it wasn't mine. Every time you get through another stage you can't believe your luck and it's an amazing warm feeling that fills your whole body. I suppose it's knowing that you're that little bit closer to the final.

Those of us who had been put through were split into groups A, B and C and told what we would be singing. Group A had to sing 'End Of The Road' by Boyz II Men – Nicholas was in that group – Group B had to sing 'I'll Be There' by the Jackson 5 and Group C had to sing 'Always On My Mind' by Elvis Presley. We were all staying in a hotel nearby and had a very short time to rehearse our songs before the next day, when we had to perform to the panel again. I can remember walking in, seeing a piano on the stage and feeling the pressure increase. When my turn came I went on stage and said 'Hi', but before I could say anything else Louis asked me to lose the cap; once it was off I started singing 'I'll Be There'. Afterwards I thought I'd sung it well, and I certainly enjoyed myself, but until they uttered those magic words, I wasn't counting my chickens. Louis finally said I was through and added that I looked like a star and sang like a star, but he said that at first he thought I looked a bit cocky. I didn't reply at the time because I was just so excited to have got through, but I'm not cocky and I didn't want him to think I was, so after that I tried my level best to prove it.

There were now only seven of us left, so it was getting pretty close to the final selection, and we were all taken over to Dublin. Each judge took the finalists in their group either to their house or to a hotel. I think Simon took his category – the groups – to a house in Spain and Sharon took hers – the over twenty-fives – to her house in LA. We went to Louis' home town, Dublin, which was fine by me, as you can imagine.

Once we were there, each of us was given one song to perform, and mine was 'The Air That I Breathe' by the Hollies. Apparently Louis wanted to challenge my voice a bit more and that's why he chose that song for me. My memories are so crystal clear that I can even remember what I was wearing that day: white Timberland boots – the heaviest shoe ever to exist – and Faye Sawyer was laughing at me. I thought she was laughing because I was dancing from side to side when I sang – I can never stand still when I'm singing – but I think it was the boots that had made her giggle. While I was singing, I did the cheesiest thing

BEFORE I COULD SAY ANYTHING ELSE LOUIS ASKED ME TO LOSE THE CAP

ever. I was singing the bit where it repeats, ' … to love you' and I pointed at Faye as I sang the line first and then at Yvie as it's repeated. All the time I was thinking, why are you being so corny Shayne? But then on the third repeat I didn't point at Louis, I put my hand down instead, and they all started laughing – I think that kind of broke the ice.

Once we'd all been in to sing we had to go back individually to get our results. I felt so sick when I walked into the room because I knew that if I wasn't chosen I'd got so close but just not quite made it – I think that would have been worse than being knocked out in one of the earlier rounds. Louis said to me, 'You look like a star and you sound like one – you are in my final four.' The words hit me slowly and my jaw hit the ground, I couldn't believe it. The feeling of having got that far against all the odds was just incredible.

I walked over to Louis and gave him the biggest hug, and as soon as I walked out I was greeted by Kate. I was so happy I started crying – it took ages for the fact that I was in the final four to sink in.

Louis and I hit it off pretty much from the start, I think mainly because of our Irish connections and our first proper conversation, which was on the balcony of the hotel we stayed at in Dublin. Yvie gave me a mug that has a picture on it of her, Faye and Louis sitting on the sofa they sat on while they were judging. I asked Louis to sign it and he drew a halo over his head – as you do! – but I guess it's better than the two-fingers 'bunny ears' he usually does behind people's backs. It sits in my kitchen above the bottle of champagne he gave me when I won. I don't use it because it captured that

moment I went through to the finals and I don't want the pen to rub off. The next day we made our way home from Ireland, and at that point none of my family knew that I had got through – I wasn't allowed to tell them because they had gathered the whole family together to wait for me at home. I was followed by a camera crew who walked with me all the way down my road to my front door. Cameras seemed to be everywhere and as walked in and looked around the sitting room all my family were staring at me, holding hands; it felt like the whole thing was happening in slow motion with all the attention on me, and all I said was, 'I'm in.' Then everyone rushed towards me and it was the best feeling in the world. Everyone was grabbing me and congratulating me and there were lots and lots of tears. I never thought I'd make it that far, so it felt like a massive achievement.

I packed a suitcase of my stuff, some clothes – jeans and T-shirts and caps – everything I felt comfortable in, plus a couple

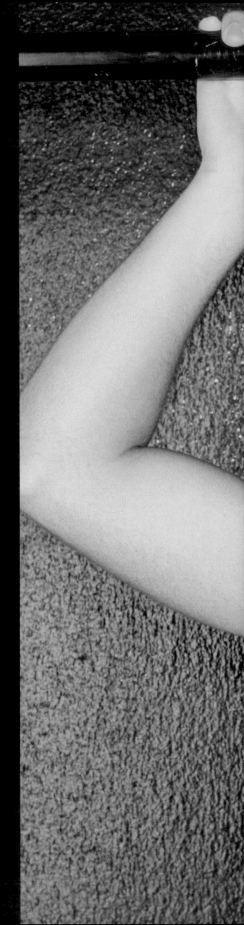

of smart outfits as well, ready for my move to the house in London. I didn't really know what to pack or what to expect, so it was quite difficult, but I made sure I had a picture of Mum and Faye with me, and once I was all packed and ready to go I was driven down south to meet the other finalists.

The first time I knew who had made it to the other categories was when we all met at the Thames building in London. I walked in and saw all the guys' faces, which was pretty weird, because so many of them looked familiar from when I'd seen them at the auditions. The first thing you think is, I knew you'd get through. The person that stuck out more than anyone was Chico – you can never forget Chico! I remember he was wearing a white jumper that really made him stand out in the crowd, and over the following weeks I got to know him really well. I don't think any of us thought he would get through on his singing alone, but he's such a fun guy you can see why Sharon wanted him in her group. Brenda was the first person I spoke to, I think, and she just turned round to me, smiled and said, 'I knew you'd be here.' Andy said the very same thing.

The conversations at the beginning were just like the normal conversations you have when you first meet people, really. We talked about the auditions and how nerve-racking they were; we talked about our jobs and how excited we were about the show and even how we were all going to do our very best every week. Probably what sticks out in my mind the most about the day we all met was talking to the Conway Sisters – they told me almost immediately that I was going to win. I didn't believe them, but the whole way through they believed in me. I had even been

tipped to win by the betting shop Paddy Power, which I think people knew, and so there was an added bit of pressure on me right from the start.

Everyone in the room looked so familiar. I didn't know their names but I recognised them, and the chatting and getting to know each other was natural but underneath you could sense the really competitive streak in us all, right from the beginning. At the end of the day all of us were competing against each other, and we all knew that, so we were kind of eyeing up our rivals – not in a nasty way, but I know that's what everyone was thinking.

My first impression of Brenda was that she was mad but lovely. She wasn't a diva, she was quite mumsy and that was nice. Andy was like the daddy of the group and the nice guy – he was always very complimentary about everyone. It's strange now looking back, because when I met 4 Tune I thought they would be my main threat and I clocked that the minute I laid eyes on them. Addictiv Ladies were the youngest girls and I got on with them straight away – it was a real shame when they got voted off in the first week because they were a lot of fun in the house. I can remember thinking that Journey South were nice blokes, two brothers, very talented. I didn't speak to Nicholas straight away when we met up, but obviously I knew him a bit better because of our time together in Dublin. I've got a great picture of him on my phone when he took his dreadlocks out – he'd kill me if I gave that picture to the press.

Chico is Chico, need I say more? He'd stand out wherever he went and he provided us with a lot of entertainment in the house. Each week, when we thought his number was up, he'd stay to fight another day. I remembered Chenai from the previous year when we'd both auditioned, and to be honest I don't really know what I thought of her at first. I had heard about Maria's voice even before I met her because the other contestants told me how good she was. I think the only voices I'd heard before that were 4 Tune, Journey South and Nicholas.

Phillip was kind of different altogether and he loved the whole Elvis thing, which I found a bit strange. He had a bit of a country connection, and I think that was his downfall in the end, as he went against Louis and ended up getting voted off quite early on.

As time went on and we spent more time together in the house in north London we got to know each other better. The house was a large three-storey property and we soon became like one big family. Although it was inevitable that people would get along with some more than others, there was never a nasty atmosphere. I think there were only a couple of rows – one between Brenda and Chenai and one between Nicholas and Phillip. The whole Brenda/Chenai thing was ridiculous. They were arguing about maturity of voices and it was horrible for everyone – in the end I went and got one of the researchers and he managed to resolve things. The researchers, Charlie, Dan, Lucy and Jess, were great and helped us so much during our time in the house, and when things like that happened they

were always there to sort it out.

I heard that Brenda was behaving like a bit of a diva as the competition went on but I never experienced it or saw it. She'd say things like, 'I'm going out for a fag, I don't care about what they say, I'm going for one.' But that was just Brenda; that's what made her the person she is.

The Addictiv Ladies were the messiest bunch in the house, I reckon, because they left their stuff everywhere, but Chico wasn't very tidy either. It was just like a student house really: there were never any clean plates and we'd end up eating cereal out of saucepans. I would like to point out though that the researchers for the 24/7 programme, who lived with us too, were really untidy and we'd often get the blame for their mess!

As the name suggests, the 24/7 team followed us around all day every day, capturing our every movement. We would get up at about 8 a.m., eat some breakfast and then start rehearsing for the next week. There was always something to do and I was never at a loose end in the house; I was always kept busy with press meetings, photo shoots and rehearsals with Ashley and my vocal coach Yvie. I can't stress enough how much Yvie helped me win that show, and looking back I worry that I didn't thank her as much as I should have done. There were so many people to thank and I feel like I missed her out a bit, because, honestly, I couldn't have done it without her. Yvie gave me the confidence to try notes I would never have dreamed of attempting, and she taught me to breathe properly; she was an inspiration. Before that I'd never had any singing lessons, so I learned a lot from her. I really need to buy her some flowers or something, because I want her to know how grateful I am, and always will be, for what she did for me.

As the week went on and each performance got closer, I could feel myself getting more and more uptight and nervous. Even after the live shows on Saturdays those feelings and nerves just wouldn't go away. You'd think it would get easier each week, but

it really didn't. When you do eventually come out on stage, it's what you've been working for, the moment you've been practising for all week, and you know you have to give it your all.

At times it was quite weird living like that, with no privacy and not a minute to yourself, but at the same time it was quite exciting and I felt a kind of freedom; we could do whatever we wanted. With twelve of us living together, scattered over three floors, it was always going to be interesting. I could call home whenever I wanted, which was great because I had my twenty-first birthday in there – it would have been odd for that to go by without talking to my family. Not seeing them all, especially Emma and Faye, was hard, but the guys in the house were great and threw me a little party. They woke me up in the morning with party poppers and cans of that stringy stuff, which they

sprayed all over me, and in the evening we had a few drinks to celebrate. I cracked open some champagne and opened my presents. Faye had sent me an iPod mini and I also got some new trainers and aftershave, so it was a nice relaxing day before the really hard work began again.

I don't think people understand how tough *X Factor* really is. You go through months of auditions and by the end you can really feel the strain. You are travelling all over the place, from one audition to another, and you see so many people being rejected. I still can't believe that there were 75,000 people to start with and that I was the one who won. I think people need to remember that before they start criticising how easy it is. I reckon established artists and acts who criticise *X Factor* should give it a go, because it's not as easy as it looks. Talent shows like that give people an opportunity they wouldn't normally get, a chance to do something with their lives. Learning new songs week in week out is tough, especially when you're not used to singing in front of an audience. The whole thing is pretty daunting and it's definitely the hardest thing I've ever done.

The first Saturday night show was really frightening. I was already being told what to wear and how I should look. I wore formal trousers and a shirt and I thought I looked quite smart – you have to like what you're wearing because that helps you feel confident, and I knew that if I looked the part I'd feel the part, too. All of us were sharing a dressing room

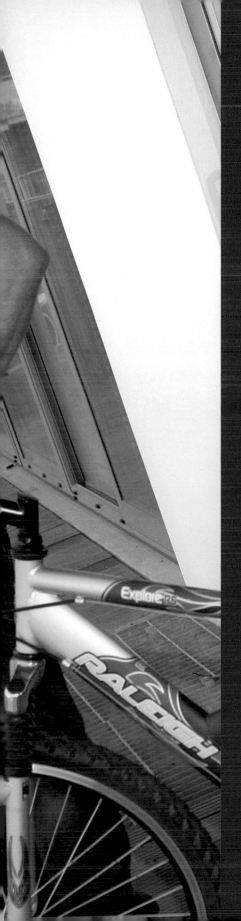

upstairs, where we changed and waited during each other's performances. For the first time in my life I had make-up put on by a make-up artist, and that was a very weird feeling. We had sound checks and rehearsals, but nothing can prepare you for singing for the first time on live TV in front of a huge audience, some of whom are waving banners and shouting your name – it was incredible. It's at the shows that you really get to know your fan base and it's a good indicator of how well liked you are. I can remember walking out on the stage for the first time and thinking, wow! You've made it. Even if I hadn't gone any further at least I'd have performed on live TV to millions of people, and that feeling was indescribable. I was singing Richard Marx's song 'Right Here Waiting' and I knew I had to really go for it or face ruining my chance of getting through. At the end the judges commented on the way I'd sung it, and in particular the pronunciation of my words because some of them had an Irish twist. They said they could see me going a long way in the competition and that boosted my confidence no end, spurring me on for the next week. I didn't really get any negative comments during the shows, the only one that was slightly negative was when I sang 'Summer of '69' and Simon felt I needed a gruff voice to do it, but that was about it. With the comments some people had I think I got off quite lightly.

My relationship with Sharon was great during the show and I think our silly banter encouraged people to tune in every week. Each time I walked on stage I would give her a little wink or something, and we kind of connected. She would do this squashing thing with her hands, indicating my err … well you know! It was really funny, but I think she got a bit of a telling off one week because she told me she had something warm and wet for me, which was thought to be a bit too rude, so the next week she covered it up by bringing out her dog! It was brilliant and Sharon is great – now when I see her I always give her a really big hug. Sharon either loves you or hates you, but fortunately she seemed to quite like me, and my brothers and sisters always wind me up about it. I don't have Mrs O's number, but I do see her quite a bit, and recently I was on a show with her. It was for her new chat show and they were filming the pilot and I was a guest. After the interview Richard Holloway and Claire Horton, the executive producers, who also produce *X Factor*, both said they thought it was a great interview and that it was really natural and comfortable. They said there was a real chemistry between us, and no tension, so I hope that when the show does go out they'll use it. My relationship with Sharon was just one long flirtation, and, I've got to be honest, I loved it. And as for Ozzy, he is fantastic. Ozzy is a very intelligent guy and they have a wicked relationship. I saw them recently at *X Factor: Battle of the Stars* show. Sharon walked out of her dressing room and saw me and her face lit up, then she saw Ozzy behind me and she lit up even more. It was so nice to see her and I hope it won't be long before we meet up again. Sharon and I have the same sense of humour, and we have a joke about our favourite scene in *Little Britain*. It's a Lou and Andy sketch and as soon as one of us says it we can't stop laughing. We always used to do it backstage and for some reason it always made us laugh. When I was nervous it was great to have an outlet and have a laugh with everyone, but I think Sharon and I had a really special bond.

I never thought I would be in the final, let alone win. People were telling me I could do it

and that once I'd sung 'Over the Rainbow' I had it in the bag, but I think if I'd believed that then I wouldn't have been standing on that stage in the final. I needed to give it my all each and every week and if I'd taken it for granted I wouldn't have won.

Louis gave me 'Over the Rainbow' to sing very early on in the competition saying, 'Shayne, I believe in you. I believe that you can get to the final.' I thought singing it was a great idea because I wanted to show the public I could be versatile. That's also why I danced when I sang Justin Timberlake's 'Cry Me A River' – I wanted to stretch myself and my performance. Some of the judges said I was staying in my comfort zone, which is fair enough, so I wanted to try and do as many different things as possible, to show my whole range. If you look back at my list of songs they were all completely different. I couldn't believe the reception I got when I sang 'Over the Rainbow', though, and sometimes now when I listen back to it and close my eyes I can

hear everyone screaming and it gives me a real buzz. When I hit
the octave slide and the high falsetto note at the very end,
everyone started to go crazy, and if you listen carefully you can
hear Louis in the background making a noise like a train going
'Wooh, wooh' – it's the funniest thing.

The weirdest time was when he phoned me when I was with
Faye just before the London shows began and we must have
been on the phone for a good hour and a half. First off he texted
me and said, 'Are you free in five. LW' and then he phoned. Can
you imagine that? Louis Walsh texting you? It was so surreal, and
as soon as I received the text I was like, 'Guess what? Louis
Walsh has just texted me!' We talked about which songs we did
and didn't like for about an hour and a half, and everything I
had on my list was more or less what he had on his. I think that's
why our working relationship is so strong: we always agree on
everything. At first he wasn't sure about me singing 'I Believe In
A Thing Called Love', but because he believed in me he didn't

I THINK SHARON AND I HAD A REALLY SPECIAL BOND

stop me. Mind you, I had to plead with him a bit, saying, 'Please, Louis, if you let me do this I will prove that I can pull it off.'

I have so much respect for Louis and I will always listen to his advice, because if you don't you'll flop. He has been instrumental in getting me this far because he believed in me from the very start. When he told me he thought I would win I couldn't believe the faith and confidence he had in me. I felt like I was the weakest in my category and that Chenai, Phillip and Nicholas would go a lot further than me. I always doubted myself and that's why when I made it to the final shows, I couldn't believe it.

During the run up to the final I think the only people who really believed in me out of all the contestants were the Conway Sisters. The house became a bit cliquey towards the end and I began to feel quite left out. People were beginning to pair up and support each other. Journey South loved Nicholas and I think everyone else was kind of behind Andy really. It was never spoken of, but you could see it. Whenever we had a sound check and everyone was listening, Andy would get a really great reception, with people singing along, clicking their fingers and swaying, and it was the same with Brenda and Maria. I just knew I had to get on with my singing and took on board all the advice I could get – from Louis, from Ashley, from Yvie and from Faye, my stylist.

My look changed a lot from the first show – my head was shaved and I had grown some 'designer' stubble. It was always going to be either me or Phillip who had their head shaved, and only one of us would get to keep the stubble – otherwise we would have the same look and style, which wouldn't benefit either of us. I didn't want to lose mine because I look so young without it, and I wanted my head shaved because if not my hair goes out of control. Ashley was really with me and Yvie that week and I nagged and nagged them both until they agreed to let me keep the stubble and lose the hair for the JT number. It worked and I was totally revamped – on live TV! I loved it.

I HAVE SO MUCH RESPECT FOR LOUIS AND I WILL ALWAYS LISTEN TO HIS ADVICE

5

READ ALL
ABOUT IT

My life started to change after my first appearance on TV, and while there was a good side to it, there was also the downside, with my personal life being splashed across the papers. The press wanted to know everything about me and suddenly I became public property.

When your last name is Ward there's always a problem, because it's a common Irish name and some Wards are known to cause trouble. Obviously there are good and bad Wards, but some people don't know the difference, and unfortunately bad Wards are known for going into pubs and smashing them up. I was often turned away from bars just because of my surname.

Reading about my family in the papers was the worst bit of my whole *X Factor* experience, and I feel dreadful that because of me they have been dragged through the press, particularly when half of what they say isn't true. It's hard to go from being a nobody to someone everyone wants to read about, and unfortunately the side effect is that things that you'd rather forget about tend to get dragged up and played out in public.

The first of those stories came out during the boot-camp stage of *X Factor*, and I found out about it by walking into the newsagent's. I think it was a Sunday tabloid that ran the story, but my stomach lurched when I saw the headline; nothing can prepare you for seeing something like that. It was about my brother Martin and it said something like '*X Factor* Contestant's Brother Accused of Murder'. It was horrible and so upsetting, not only for me, but more for my brother, who had been cleared of all charges. Martin went through hell at that time and had been remanded in custody for over a year before being released,

EVEN IF I KNOW THE STORIES ARE BEING WRITTEN I REFUSED TO READ THEM

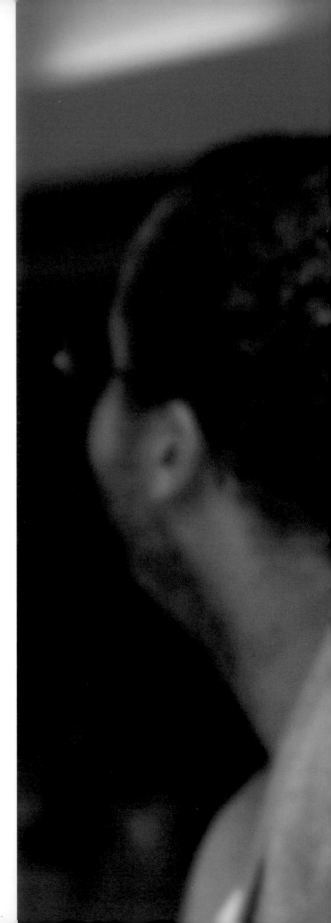

and I felt really guilty because now he was having to live through it all again. It was an unfortunate time for him, but he didn't do it and the guy who did was eventually brought to justice. Naturally, Martin wants to get on with his life, so stories like that really hurt. As soon as I found out about the story I called him to tell him about it and to apologise. Martin said he felt he couldn't show his face, but I told him he had nothing to hide and to hold his head up high because he hadn't done anything; he was just in the wrong place at the wrong time. The papers laid into him even though he had been acquitted and I can't tell you how guilty I felt. Martin spent a lot of time inside for something he didn't do, and he used to cry every night at the time. I kept thinking if I hadn't entered the competition then none of this would ever have come out. I apologised over and over and told him it would be chip paper in the morning, but as time has gone by I've seen how the media works and I know that it doesn't end there. The story gets picked up by magazines and soon it's everywhere, so in the end I decided not to search out the stories about me and my family in the papers any more. Even if I knew the stories were being written, I wouldn't read them.

A story about my dad being in prison didn't come out until I had made it into the house and on to the show. I was taken away and spoken to by Ashley, and the ITV press officers Sara Lee and Ben Webster, and pre-warned about what would be in the papers the next day; while I was away the other contestants

I KNEW THE MINUTE I WALKED BACK INTO THE ROOM THAT THEY ALL KNEW

were also told. I knew the minute I walked back into the room that they all knew, and one by one they came over and hugged me, told me not to worry and that they were all there for me. I thanked all of them because I knew that when the paper came out it would make horrible reading. I then phoned my mum to tell her myself because I knew it would upset her. None of us wanted our name dragged through the mud and it didn't seem fair. The papers wrote hardly any stories about the other contestants; there was the odd kiss 'n' tell but that was about it. I was the only person to have those sorts of stories published, and I put it down to my surname again. It's because I'm a Ward. I guess I knew in my heart of hearts that it would turn up somewhere, and that they only published it because it would sell papers, but that doesn't prepare you, believe me.

When the story about my dad came out I hadn't been in touch with him for ages, and I suppose I'd blanked a lot of it from my mind, which meant I hadn't told Louis, Ashley, Sara and Ben about it. Dad's in prison and that's the bottom line. It

I AM ME

isn't long until he gets out, but the horrible thing is that when he does get out the papers will try and find him and he will be splashed all over them again.

I haven't written my dad off, but I don't want to visit him and I don't have any contact. Out of all the stories that were written that was the worst one because it was true. It was a horrific thing that he did; he knows he did wrong. He recognises what I have achieved and I know that he was watching me inside and that he shouted as loud as he could, 'That's my son' when I won. I don't think what he has done affects me – I am me and I'm different from him. He committed a crime and he's being punished. His wife is standing by him and I don't know what the future holds, but he is always going to be there. I don't know if I'll see him when he comes out – I haven't decided whether that is something I want to do or not but I do know what people would think if I did go and see him.

People often ask me how I've turned out the way I have and I think it's down to my mum and the fact that I have a good head on my shoulders. Seeing articles about my family is really gut-wrenching and makes me feel physically sick, but I try and turn the negatives into positives and that helps me to focus even harder on proving to people that even though these things have happened I'm not going to let them hold me back or stop me from doing well. Everyone's family has some trouble in their past, but I love my family and you just have to live with what life deals you.

The only other upsetting story was when my mum got arrested just before the final, and the papers had a field day with that one. Again I was told about it before it came out, but coming just before the final, it wasn't easy to deal with. It was really hard to stay focused and not worry about her, but fortunately my fans stood by me and kept me going till the end.

I take a lot of what I read with a pinch of salt now and I think if I didn't it would affect me a lot more, which obviously I don't want because I'm focusing on my career now. I don't want to know about stories of uncles in prison and all that – I don't even know them and they have nothing to do with me. It's as if everyone with the surname Ward is connected to me, which is ridiculous.

Sometimes, though, I have to admit, the papers come up with some funny headlines. One I remember well was 'Shayne is a Role Model for the ASBO Generation'. That was hilarious and had me in stitches. In general my press coverage has been good and bad, so you have to take the rough with the smooth and I guess it must have helped, because here I am now and the overwhelming memories of the great times will never disappear. Like the final time I stood in front of the *X Factor* audience, on live TV, waiting a lifetime to hear the words that would confirm I had achieved my wildest dream, my goal.

6

X MARKS
THE NUMBER
ONE SPOT

Standing on the stage on final night, in front of my fans, my family and what felt like the world, will live with me for ever. As will hearing, 'Shayne Ward. Congratulations! You are the winner of *X Factor* 2005.'

I can't put into words what the moment felt like when Kate said my name, but it was, I imagine, like winning the biggest lottery rollover ever. Everything moved in slow motion and every sound was blocked out apart from Kate's voice. I have a picture of the moment framed on my living-room wall – it completely captures the relief, amazement and sheer happiness. And Louis was there by my side, feeling it too. I was in so much shock I was not just crying – tears were streaming down my face, on live TV! Andy was hugging Sharon as I went over to him to say sorry. He congratulated me, but it must have been hard to get so close and then have all your dreams dashed at the very last moment. As excited as I was, I really felt for him and his family in the audience; after all it easily could have been me, and I know I would have been devastated.

I looked into the audience to see my family, who had been there supporting me each and every week. They were going crazy, they were so excited. My mum, my sisters, my brothers, Faye and my mates Gareth and Ben were all there, screaming at the tops of their voices, and I had to keep reminding myself that we were still being filmed. It was mental and to see them that happy just made me even happier. Every week they had watched other contestants' families go home filled with disappointment when they were voted off, and I didn't want that. I know that other people's families have had bad times but over the years my family has constantly struggled and had it really hard, so I wanted some happiness for them, and no matter what, I didn't want them to leave disappointed.

All I wanted to do was run over and hug them, and even when Kate said, 'You've won, how do you feel? Is this all for your mum?' All I could get out of my mouth was 'Yes, it's all for my mum.' I was so shocked I could hardly string a sentence together. I was bowled over by it all, and although my mind was racing with questions about what I would have to do next, for those few minutes I was quite happy to enjoy the moment and the madness surrounding me. Kate then told me to look up at the big screen, which was rigged up on the stage. I looked up and Andi Peters was standing there saying, 'This is your first debut single being made.' He was beside a huge machine in the CD factory and had pressed a button to start making my single 'That's My Goal'. It was a lot to take in, not only had I won but my first single was being made. I had been so focused on the competition I had forgotten that was part of

the show and seeing it happen left me in even more shock. Kate was saying to me, 'Look, Shayne, this is for you.' But instead of reacting I was looking at my mum saying, 'I can't believe it, I can't believe it. I did this for you; this is all for you.' I think my brain just switched off and poor Kate had to repeat nearly every question before she got an answer out of me. I remember looking at Louis, my family and then up at the big screen and Andi Peters, and the sense of pride and disbelief was written all over my face. When I watch it back now I look like a rabbit caught in the headlights, not knowing where to look or where to go. I was so, so happy, and although it sounds corny, for me, winning *X Factor* has been, and is, the best thing that has ever happened to me and my family. It has opened the door to a new future for us all, one where, hopefully, I can take all my mum's worries away, and for that reason the moment Kate announced me as the winner goes down as being the happiest moment of my life. I've had a permanent grin on my face ever since – even now, as I'm writing, I'm beaming from ear to ear ...

My life hasn't stopped since the day I won. Little did I know that 17 December 2005 would be the day my life changed beyond recognition. Everything, and I mean everything, is different. I hardly recognise myself when I look back to my life before, and I don't think anyone can prepare themselves for that. I knew things would be different, but never in my wildest dreams did I think it could be as amazing as this. When the show finished I was whisked off to do the ITV2 show *Xtra Factor* with Ben Shepherd – all the guys were up there in the studio waiting for me and the cheers made me feel like a king. Out of all the twelve people with amazing voices sitting on the couch, I was the one who had won. I still find it hard to comprehend. You can imagine my head was everywhere at that point, just after finding out. I had a short amount of time to see my family and Faye after that interview with Ben but it wasn't long because there were so many people to see and I was so

knocked still I didn't know who I was speaking to. If you asked me now who I met that night I'd be hard pushed to tell you. I was walking on air and in a bubble that no one could burst. I know I had a drink with Louis, Ashley and Yvie in Louis' dressing room afterwards; Louis was so excited and the feeling, the buzz, backstage was incredible. Time seemed to go by really quickly as it all sank in and before I knew it I was being whisked off to perform at the massive London nightclub G-A-Y.

Each week, when someone was knocked out of the competition, they would be whisked away after the Saturday night show to sing at the club, and finally it was my turn. I didn't really know what to expect and I didn't know if anyone there had been watching or knew that I had won, but Jeremy Joseph, who runs the club, introduced me on to the stage as the winner of *X Factor* 2005 and when I walked on I couldn't believe the reception: it was out of this world. It was brilliant because everyone was cheering my name and going crazy. When you're in the house you're kept away from fans, you do some personal appearances and things but you don't have any idea how big you are becoming. I imagine it's a bit like *Big Brother* when you just don't know how you are being received by the outside world. I was too busy concentrating on getting through each week so my mind didn't even go there. People would say to me things like, 'Shayne, you don't realise how big you are,' but I didn't believe them and would just say, 'Yeah, yeah don't be silly.' So to walk out on that stage and get that kind of a welcome was a huge, huge shock. It's a weird sensation going from walking down the street without being noticed to everyone knowing who you are. People started to shout my name across the street and I would laugh, thinking, you don't know me!

I got back to the house really late after G-A-Y. I'd been so excited that I sung my heart out on stage and, with hindsight, pushed myself way too hard so my voice suffered the consequences. I only had a few hours' sleep, partly because I was so excited and partly because I had to be up to do interviews. For the next four days I did them solidly. The first one was with the *Sun*, which I think came out on the Monday morning, and I talked about winning and had my picture taken, and I later went back to edit their showbiz column. It was constant – there were three interviews after that with radio stations, and in the afternoon *Top of the Pops*. I'd never been on that side of the press before and hadn't done much media training, but I knew I had to be careful – try and not say anything to embarrass myself! – as it was all new to me.

When I appeared on *Top of the Pops*, the day after the final of *X Factor*, it still hadn't sunk in that I'd won, even though my lifestyle was already changing drastically. I had security for a start, cars to drive me around and even my own dressing room with 'Shayne Ward' on the door. During the weeks of singing at Fountain Studios, where *X Factor* is filmed, I had become more and more used to performing in front of an audience. Don't get me wrong, I was always very nervous, my mouth would feel dry before I walked on stage and my hands would feel slightly sweaty, and if I let my

mind think about how big a deal the show was I would really freak out.

I was performing 'That's My Goal' on *Top of the Pops*, and I was desperate for it to be the Christmas number one. I kept thinking how amazing it would be to hit the top spot with my first single and make my mum the proudest mum in the world, but at the same time I was trying not to get my hopes up as I knew there was stiff competition. It was about 11 a.m. and I was waiting in my dressing room at the BBC for a call to go on. I was nervous and excited all at once.

There were a few of us just sitting round chatting. Paul Higgins, who looks after me for security – how weird is that! – Dan Parker, my sycho product manager, and I were talking about the show when there was a knock on the door. I shouted, 'Come in,' and in walked Robbie Williams. Our jaws dropped. I thought he might have walked into the wrong room, but before I knew what was happening I said: 'All right, Rob!' And in the most bizarre sequence of events Rob looked at me and shouted, 'Come here.' He then gave me the biggest hug ever, congratulated me and said, 'Well done!' My mind was working overtime as I wondered how the hell he knew who I was. I thought, here I am at *Top of the Pops*, in my own dressing room, with my own security, and Robbie Williams is congratulating me. I was pinching myself – it was like one big dream and I thought at any minute I would wake up. I felt kind of numb as Rob explained to me that he had been watching *X Factor* in LA and that he'd been backing me all the way. It turned out that he had been supporting me since the beginning and really wanted me to win. I don't know if he voted for me, but he was definitely on my side, so I guess he might have done. I was so chuffed and totally bowled over by it all, but I was convinced that someone must have asked him to come in and see me and that it was staged, so I asked him. He assured me that he wanted to come and that no one had asked him. He said, 'I heard you were here and wanted to come in of my own accord and say congratulations.' That meant a massive deal to me.

Although I had met celebrities on the show, to know that the Robbie Williams had been supporting me and had come to find me and congratulate me was pretty special. About three weeks before I met Rob, Kate Thornton told me that he had been asking after me and that he wanted to know whether I played football. To be honest I didn't really believe her. I think I was so wrapped up in the show and trying my hardest to get to the final that it kind of went in one ear and out of the other. I couldn't get my head around the fact that someone that famous was asking after me – I still can't! While we were in the dressing room we talked about all sorts of things, in particular *X Factor* and having a career in the music industry, and Rob was giving me advice. He told me that people had been approaching him in the street, saying they could see a bit of him in me, and even he said he thought the same and that we have similar personalities. He gave me so much encouragement, telling me that he could see me doing really well. He also told me the road to success is not an easy one and that I would have to work really hard, but that if I gave it my all I would go far. I really respect Robbie and hope that one day I can achieve as much. I guess Kate wasn't fibbing after all, because he also mentioned the football. He asked me if I would like to have a game and of course I said yes. It turned out that Rob wanted me to be part of his team for Soccer

Aid, but unfortunately I couldn't do it because I was working on the album – I was absolutely gutted.

Just before Rob left we swapped numbers – how crazy is that? – and agreed to keep in contact. It seemed like we'd been chatting for ages, when in reality it wasn't that long. I think the other people in the dressing room were as shocked as me – their faces were a picture. I was so made up afterwards that I went out on stage and gave it my all. I performed 'That's My Goal' with my own choir, which was pretty cool, and the whole place erupted, cheering for me. Everyone was going mad, especially the girls, which I quite liked. I knew from the previous weeks in the studio on *X Factor* they went crazy but to see the public's reaction in another studio was quite amazing and surreal.

The next time Robbie's and my paths crossed was when I had a virus on my mobile phone. It was during the *X Factor* tour and my mobile was sending everyone dodgy text messages saying 'Subject: Porn, Sender: Shayne'. No one could open the message – it was just a virus – but that didn't stop me getting loads of calls from people asking me why I was sending them porn. Rob must have received one because he sent a message back saying, 'Who is this?' I was so embarrassed and it took me ages to try and work out how to explain to him what had happened. Eventually I texted back apologising for the message and tried to tell him about the problem with my mobile. Luckily he wasn't bothered and told me not to worry. I knew he couldn't have been too annoyed because he asked me how my album was going and said that he hoped I was well and we could catch up soon.

Of course the story about the porn texts turned up in the papers. It's kind of strange reading about yourself in the media. It's something I don't think I'll ever get used to or be comfortable with, but it's just the way it is and I have to accept that. Fortunately the text story was fairly harmless, and for once it was pretty accurate, although how they found out about it I'll

Not long afterwards Rob was back in the UK to do some promotion and we were hoping to meet up, but unfortunately, yet again, we couldn't, although I'm sure at some point our schedules will allow it. I haven't ever rung him because I feel a bit awkward; I mean, I know him because I've met him but it was only once and I'm not the kind of person to ring up someone I don't really know. I'm quite shy when it comes to things like that and I just wouldn't feel comfortable. To be honest it does feel a bit odd as I've somehow been shoved in at the deep end when it comes to meeting famous people. Of course I get nervous and I don't think it will ever feel normal mixing in those circles, but I hope I'm getting better at it. My mum always tells me that everyone is human, no matter what their background, job or lifestyle, and I try to remember her words whenever I get star struck – although my heart still jumps in to my mouth when I see Sharon!

Appearing on the last Christmas *Top of the Pops* was incredible, a real privilege. And no sooner had I done that I had another early start the following day to appear on GMTV, where I sang 'That's My Goal' again. After that I met Lorraine Kelly and was interviewed on her show, but to be honest it's all a bit hazy now. I had hardly slept after the excitement of TOTP and I was just running on adrenaline, having a massive buzz. I just thought, what is going on here? I was literally being driven from one place to another to appear on as many shows and radio stations as possible – it was mad.

I absolutely loved doing the main shows like Chris Moyles on Radio 1, and going back to Manchester and being on my local radio station was massive for me because it was broadcast all across my city, which was an incredible feeling. There is nothing quite like going back to your home town and giving something back when you've made it big, because you have so much support there, so that was definitely my favourite bit.

Two days after the final – and lots of interviews later – an *X Factor* wrap party was thrown for all the contestants, presenters and production staff. It was so good to see everyone again, although I already felt like I was being treated differently. For a start I was being chauffeured around. My time wasn't really my own any more and I had people around me telling me what to do and when to do it. It was a great party, with everyone getting smash drunk, and we watched loads of the shows' out takes, which were funny, but I was gutted because I had an early start the next day and they wouldn't let me stay. I kept saying, 'I can't leave this early,' and nagging them, but in the end I got dragged home to bed. I really wanted to stay and party, and I couldn't help but wonder what the other guys thought when I left.

I went back to Manchester on the 21 December, just before Christmas and two days after the wrap party. It was such a weird feeling being back at home after all that. One minute you're a celebrity in London and the next you're back in your bedroom at home. In London I was treated differently but when I got home my family were exactly the same, which was really refreshing. This downtime gave me an opportunity to reflect on what had happened over the last few days and the whirlwind I had been living through.

Christmas Day was lovely; all the family came round to our house and we gave each other presents. I bought Faye a nice chain and Lisa helped me out with everyone else's pressies. She's always good at that and we usually go halves.

The thing that stands out most about Christmas Day last year, though, was 'That's My Goal' going to number one. We all sat there waiting in the living room because the Radio 1 *Chart Show* was counting down and we wanted to hear it. I knew it was going to be at the top spot because I'd got a call to tell me the sales were really good, but I wanted to hear it for myself. It was such a surreal moment: I was standing in the doorway listening to the countdown and when they got to the top five I walked to the front door with a bottle of champagne, then when they announced it was number one I went outside, popped the cork and screamed as loud as I could – the moment kind of overtook me. It brought back the win all over again, bringing tears to my eyes, and we all started dancing around the house. All the family were there, my sisters, my brothers and all their kids, but most importantly my mum and it made her so proud. Afterwards we turned on the telly to watch *Top of the Pops*, and it was so strange to see myself on the box performing. I know I keep saying over and over how amazing it all was, but it just happened so fast: from me having a regular job in Manchester, with a family that had always struggled, to winning a talent show, having a Christmas number one and singing on *Top of the Pops*. I don't think words can really describe how that felt for any of us.

Once it was official, my phone rang constantly. First it was Sonny Takhar, Simon's right-hand man and vice president of my record label, saying congratulations – both Sonny and Simon sent me two bottles of Cristal as a well done. Ashley called me from his holiday and I remember him saying, 'Enjoy

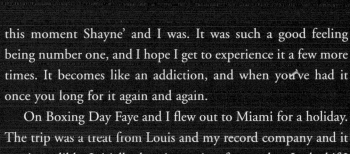

this moment Shayne' and I was. It was such a good feeling being number one, and I hope I get to experience it a few more times. It becomes like an addiction, and when you've had it once you long for it again and again.

On Boxing Day Faye and I flew out to Miami for a holiday. The trip was a treat from Louis and my record company and it was incredible. Initially the trip was just for me, but I asked if I could take Faye along because she really deserved a break, too, and I wanted to spend some time with her. We flew out there first class, which was a real experience – there was champagne and everything. Before that I'd only ever been to Spain and Turkey, so for me it was like paradise. Faye and I were loving it. We stayed for a week and it was great to have some time together and, apart from one paparazzi, we were pretty much left alone. The pictures the paparazzi took turned up in the press a couple of days later and poor Faye hates them. Mind you, I can't say I liked them that much – I was really tucking into a burger at the time and look like a right pig. I would never release a picture of the two of us; I don't ever want to become known as a media-hungry couple. After such a long time apart the trip was just what we needed as we got time to cuddle up and be a normal couple again. Louis was out there at the same time because he has a place there, but we hadn't arranged to meet up or anything so I couldn't believe it when Faye and I were out shopping one day and we saw him in a bookshop.

After we'd bumped into Louis we organised to go out to dinner. I can't remember the name of the restaurant, but it was very swanky and there were photographers everywhere – not for us, though, Leonardo DiCaprio was in town and apparently he was eating at the same restaurant. At first I thought all the flashing was some kind of strobe effect; it was only when Faye said that Leonardo was right behind us that I realised the paps were out in force. He was wearing a cap so as not to be noticed – no chance. Later the press reported that I

THERE IS NOTHING QUITE LIKE GOING BACK TO YOUR HOME TOWN

went out and had a drink with him, but in reality I just saw him walk in and that was it! – just goes to show you can't believe everything you read in the papers …

Life is still passing by at a 100 miles an hour, with new things for me to do each day, and every time I think I've got a week off to relax something else crops up. But I can't complain because I'm living my dream; I'm having some great experiences and I have met so many lovely people. Being photographed and interviewed is a lot of fun and one of my first proper shoots was for *Heat*. I was dressed up to look like Jack from *Lost* and when I saw it in print I was amazed. I was dressed exactly like him, posing on a beach looking up at the sun just after the plane crash. Louis phoned me up and said, 'Wow! You look amazing.' I must admit they did a great job and we did look really alike – I could hardly recognise myself.

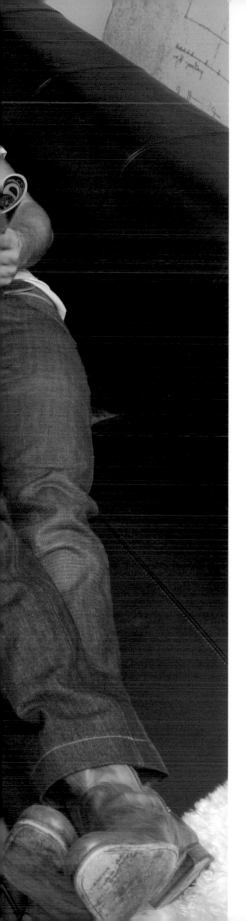

They also did Kate Thornton dressed up as the *X Factor* judges and David Walliams and Matt Lucas as Peter and Jordan, which was hilarious – I would love to meet those two at some point. At least I got be a cool, good-looking character – it did wonders for the street cred!

That's about the only shoot I've done for a magazine, apart from recently when I did *Attitude*. I can't believe the gay following I have and the interviewer was quite hard on me asking whether I had ever considered swapping teams, but I kept repeating: 'I'm afraid it's a "no".' Don't get me wrong, I have lots of gay friends who I love dearly, but there is no way I'm ever going there. I like the ladies, thank you. The rest of my work has mainly been TV promotional work like *CD:UK*, and that was brilliant but sad at the same time because it was the last show ever on ITV. I used to watch *CD:UK* when I was younger and I couldn't believe it was coming to an end, but at least I got to perform on it before it did. They had two big pictures of me and a picture of my album cover. That was the first time I had seen my album cover and it was a real defining moment for me. Even then I was still in shock – I kept pinching myself and walking around thinking, this doesn't seem real, I can't believe that this is my life.

After that it was *X Factor: Battle of the Stars*, and on final night I sang my single 'Stand By Me'. It was really odd going back to Fountain Studios and performing on that stage again. All my nerves came back and Louis had to keep settling me, saying, 'Don't worry, don't worry, you have won, you know.' But that didn't stop it feeling like the final all over again and I got pretty stressed. Sharon was really funny on that show and, true to form, if she has something to say she just says it. When she said to Rebecca Loos, 'Next time, keep your knickers on, it might warm up your voice box, and nice boob job,' I think everyone was shocked but it was a great TV moment and all I can say is that I'm very glad she likes me!

7

TOURING
AND BEYOND

I want to make a special mention of my minder Paul Higgins, who so far hasn't been mentioned in anyone's book, apart from being referred to as a tour manager. Louis has known him for ages and they're both Irish, so need I say more? Paul has tour-managed for loads of different acts, including Girls Aloud and security for Westlife. He has his own firm and will provide security for anyone. Louis phoned up Paul well before I won and told him that he had the winner – that's how much confidence Louis had in me – and he told Paul he wanted him to work with me. Paul was like, 'Who is this guy?' He hadn't seen me perform before so he didn't know what Louis was on about, but after that he watched the show and said he was really pleased because he thought it would be like the Westlife days all over again. Fingers crossed it will be, because Westlife started out slow and built up to become massive.

I first met Paul during the semi-finals of *X Factor* and since then he has looked after and tour-managed me. I have really gained a friend in Paul and he has been fantastic to me. I remember at the beginning my mum turning round to him and saying, 'Look after my son, won't you?' and I don't think he wanted to mess with her so he always has. He is such a nice guy and I don't like referring to Paul as my driver or a tour manager or security as he is a friend, and a good one at that. He has never sold out and is a truly genuine guy – if anyone asks me who he is I just say the most important thing, he is my mate.

Paul comes with me pretty much everywhere I go. I can go to places on my own if I want to, but I prefer not to because I don't think it's sensible – anything could happen because you don't know what nutters are out there. After all, there were a lot of people who didn't like me during *X Factor*. Mum has been receiving hate mail about me since, telling me to watch my back and saying that I shouldn't have won, and if people are willing to take the time to write letters like that, what else are they capable of? I don't want to put myself in the position of finding out. It's horrible but you just have to rise above it. Yes it hurts, but if you let it get you down then they've won, and we would never let that happen.

My family focused on me throughout *X Factor* while I focused on the show. I want to put that in this book because I often get asked how my family feel about all the stories that have appeared in the press. The answer is that we don't let it bother us – you just can't. You will always get jealous people.

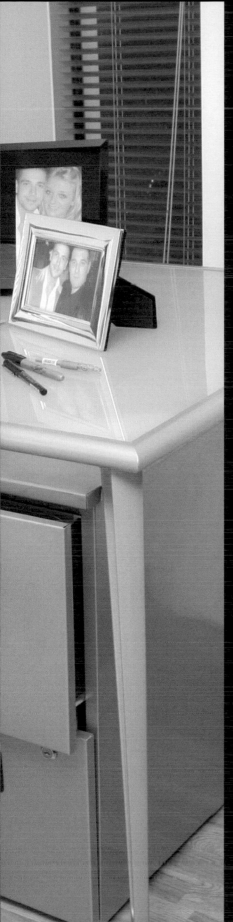

My mum has gone to the police about the hate mail she's received, but she isn't frightened – we are too strong for that. The only thing we worry about is each other.

Not long after I won I found out that I had a nodule on my throat. A nodule is when your vocal chord rips slightly – it turns out that my enthusiasm at G-A-Y pushed my voice too hard and I tore the chord. The thing is I was so excited that night after the win that I just sang my heart out and I pushed myself too far. I was screaming to the fans and the next morning I was really hoarse. I was totally devastated when I found out and I completely panicked. I had to go to the doctor's and have a camera put down my nose and throat, and it was really unpleasant. I tried to rest my voice and drink lots of water so i could avoid the laser, but at the same time my main worry was that i could be pulled off the *X Factor* tour because of it. I was adamant that wouldn't happen. I had won the show and I needed to be there. In the end they agreed, but on the understanding that I pre-recorded some of the songs so my voice had a chance to rest. But even when I'm supposed to mime I don't and that's the problem. I just get carried away and sing along anyway. I found it really hard to mime, to be honest, and that's why the nodule has caused me problems. I just want people to know how much I want to perform for them, regardless of the nodule and the pain it causes, so much so that I've been risking my voice.

The reason I'm explaining this is because I want people to know how much I hate miming. Things have to be really bad for me to mime on stage, and I hope people understand that I would rather mime now while I'm healing and have a career than ruin my vocal chords for ever. I still want to go out there and put on a live show, and it's really frustrating not to be able to do that. On the tour I sang 'Over the Rainbow' one night, and at the end Brenda and Andy came over and said they were really proud of me for doing it. I felt like saying, thanks for being proud, but you guys have got your full voices and every night I'm singing over my laid-down tracks. I may have had a nodule but I'm still going out there trying to give it 100 per cent. I know they all thought I was miming, but I wasn't, and as much as I respect them I was sensitive about it.

Chico compered the show while we were on tour. He would go on and perform his songs, and then every so often he'd go back on stage to give the crowd a competition or something. He was really good at it. On tour the Conways got booed quite a bit, and I asked Chico to say something to the crowd because the Conways didn't deserve it. I asked him to tell the crowd they were there to enjoy themselves and that the Conways were also there to enjoy themselves, not to be booed. Chico went on and said it, and when he came off the Conways thanked him. It just seemed the right thing to do and I hope it helped them enjoy the performance.

The *X Factor* tour was incredible and it was, I guess, my first proper concert where I got to meet fans across the country. We toured all over – Manchester, London, Scotland – and we all stayed in the same hotel so were with each other more or less all the time. When I walked into the hotel and saw Nicholas, Brenda, Phillip and the Conway sisters', it was just brilliant – it was like we were a family again and like being back in the house. I think my days in the *X Factor* house were some of the best times I've had in ages and I was hoping the tour would be the same. I guess it's natural for people to be more friendly with some than others but I did feel as though some people had favourites and I sort of felt left out. That probably wasn't helped by our travel arrangements. It was a bit weird really because the guys would travel on a coach together while I was driven by Paul in the Range Rover. I worried that the others might be annoyed by the fact that I was travelling separately and it kind of singled me out and made me feel quite isolated. I don't think people

I THINK MY DAYS IN THE *X FACTOR* HOUSE WERE SOME OF THE BEST TIMES I'VE HAD

minded and they understood I had other commitments during the tour. I don't think they thought it was me being funny, because at times I really wanted to travel on the coach, I just had to be in the car to do all the things on my schedule. If someone else had won it would have been the same for them, but I felt like they were bonding more because of it and I missed out on the fun of travelling together.

Despite all of that the tour was brilliant and I really enjoyed myself – we would all gear each other up before we went on stage, and when we came off we'd stand and support whoever was on next. It was great fun and the reception we got from the audience was amazing. It was the first real contact I'd had with the fans since my appearance at G-A-Y, so I was really unsure what it would be like. At the start of each tour in a different city we'd walk on stage – the girls on one side and the boys on the other – and criss-cross each other. The reception was amazing; the audience would raise the roof with their screams and I'm still amazed by it now. It was incredible to have such support from our fans.

I've had so many amazing experiences since I won that I don't know which was the best one: I'm overwhelmed by them all. I think if I had to choose it would have to be the *X Factor* tour because of

the incredible support I got from the fans everywhere we went. If I got a standing ovation I was just blown away, and it gave me so much confidence, especially in Manchester, where we all got an even better reception than anywhere else.

The *X Factor* rejects travelled everywhere with us and the guy I got on with the best had to be Robert Thompson – we had such a laugh together. His favourite saying was, 'Take me to the pod,' and at the end he gave me a T-shirt with all our names on it, signed 'Take me to the pod'. The saying comes from when he sang 'Be My Girl' to the judges and after he'd finished he walked out to the camera and said it was a resounding No, No, No, then he said, 'Take me to the pod,' which is where you go afterwards to express your feelings. He says it in such a dead serious way that it's hilarious. He's such a nice guy but I haven't seen him for a while, which is a shame; it would be great to keep in touch.

The little guy – Sumon Sanyal who sang 'Touch My Fire' – would dance crazily each night and I would wind him up saying, 'Tonight's the night you need to do something a bit special.' One night he walked out on stage with a towel round himself pretending he was naked. He then threw it off and into the crowd, along with little pieces of paper he'd ripped up, pretending they were rose petals. It was hilarious! On the final night of the tour we geared him up to do something really mad, saying it was the final night and that he had to give it his all if he wanted to be noticed. It was a bit mean but very funny. I told him there was a talent spotter in the audience and that he really needed to strut his stuff if he wanted to be picked up. And he did, he properly went for it, going totally mad. He was running around with paper and balloons – I think at one stage security even tried to get him off but they couldn't catch him. I don't know whether he got talent spotted, but he certainly entertained us every night. Who knows, perhaps Simon or Louis would like to sign him?! He kind of brought the group together really because we'd all gather round to watch him. When all the rejects came on to sing 'My Way' we would stand there, creasing up with laughter watching them. They were brilliant and loved every moment of the show. It was the funniest part of the night and the crowd laughed just as much as us all.

After the shows we would go back to our hotel and have a drink in the bar, relax a bit and catch up with everyone. We would stay up until about two or three in the morning just winding down. It's such a buzz being on stage that when you come back you're still on a high and there's no way you can sleep when you feel like that.

I have had a pretty gruelling schedule since *X Factor* finished – I think most people have. Initially it was, boom! You're doing this, then this, then that. But now I have a more planned diary, so at least I know in advance what I am doing. It's still massively busy but this way I know when I can get to have a lie-in and look forward to it.

It was during the tour that the money started to come in, and my first big splurge was a house for my mum. It was so rewarding to be able to buy her something she has always wanted and deserved. My mum had been house hunting and had found and fallen in love with a place in Manchester, but I told her it had been sold and she'd have to find something else. I knew she was really disappointed, but I was only winding her up as I had bought it without her knowing. When she came to see me on tour I got all my brothers and sisters together in my dressing room and said, 'Can I have silence, please. Mum, I have something that you really want. I've been keeping it a secret for quite some time and I know you really want it and I think you know what it is.' She mouthed the words, 'The house' and I said, 'Yes, I've bought it and it's yours.' She ran over and jumped up – it was the best moment. The feeling I got from being able to do that for her was

I PICKED HER UP AND SPUN HER AROUND AS SHE BURST INTO TEARS

incredible. Everyone was clapping and I picked her up and spun her around as she burst into tears. She kept saying thank you and I just said you're welcome because finally I was able to give something back to her.

I pay the mortgage each month, which means Mum doesn't have anything to worry about financially, and my sisters who live with her pay rent, so she has money to live on, and when I get money I send her a cheque or put money in her account. I remember the first time I did that she couldn't believe it; her whole face lit up like a picture. She is so grateful but really it's me who should be grateful.

I started recording the album not long after the *X Factor* tour finished, and it was a fairly quick turnaround, so I was kept very busy for a few weeks in the recording studio. It was a fantastic experience having my own songs written for me and recording in state-of-the-art studios – slightly different from my days on the music programme in Manchester. For a start half the album was recorded in Sweden.

Once it was all done and we were happy with the finished article, the promotional work started, including an album launch party, which was a free concert for 15,000 fans. It was held in Manchester's Albert Square and I sang six songs. I wasn't nervous really, I was just grateful that so many people came to support me and the new album. There's something about performing in your home town that you just can't beat – a sense of pride, I think – and there really is no better feeling. Following the set there was a victory parade and a civil reception, where I received a Manchester Making It Happen award, which I've put up on my wall at home. It meant so much to me to win an award in my own town and it was a really special day.

Fortunately the album did really well. It was released on 17 April 2006, Easter Monday, and went straight to number one. I think it sold something like 200,000 in the first week, which is a real achievement and gave me a lot of confidence. I don't

think even in my wildest dreams I could have imagined that happening. I joked beforehand that if it didn't do well I would have to get another job, but luckily it did so that won't be happening just yet. I was thrilled to reach number one with my debut album, and when I look at some of the people who've come through these competitions and not been so fortunate, it makes me feel even more grateful.

The videos for my singles have also been great fun to make. There have been so many incredible moments it's hard to know where to begin. The first video was for 'No Promises', and we shot in LA with top director Joseph Khan. I didn't know who he was at first so I Googled him and it was only then that I realised what great stuff he's done. There are five or six top music video directors, and he is one of them; he's directed Britney Spears, George Michael, the Backstreet Boys and Eminem's videos, so I was well chuffed to be working with him. I think the realisation that I was on the road to making it hit me at that point, because working with someone like him is an amazing opportunity many artists don't get.

The video was based on the film *Ghost* starring Demi Moore and Patrick Swayze and I literally followed Joseph's instructions to the letter as it was all so new to me. It was freezing cold and we were filming outside, but I was so excited I didn't really care what the temperature was. We did one scene where I was leaning against the bar singing and I heard Joseph say, 'Yes, that's it, do it again, do it again.' I didn't know what I had done; I thought it was some kind of head move or something like that, so I put my posing face on and sang the part again and almost straight away he said, cut. Then he showed me what he'd meant. Basically, because it was so cold you could see my breath when I sang, which looked really realistic given that is was based on *Ghost*. Originally they were going to add it in with special effects, but it had happened naturally and looked pretty spooky.

Ali, the girl in the video, was American and had done some

I'D NEVER DONE A LONG-HAUL FLIGHT, SO THE TRIP TO LA WAS SOMETHING ELSE

modelling before, but had never been in a music video. She had auditioned for the part and I think she was really shocked to get it because when I met her she was quite nervous. Joseph said he had chosen her because as a model she was used to posing, and he was right because she's really beautiful and we worked really well together. She's actually engaged to a police officer in the States, and despite the rumours, nothing went on. For the sake of the video, though, it was important that we looked like a couple, and there was some chemistry there, which I think came across.

Apart from my holiday in Miami with Faye, I'd never done a long-haul flight, so the trip to LA was something else. I flew first class again, which was a real treat. I had a seat that turned into a bed, so I thought, right, when I wake up I'll be in LA. Travelling like that makes all the difference because when you arrive you feel really fresh and ready to go, which was good because we only had two days to shoot the video. However, I'd like to add that I don't always fly first class – it's good to keep it real and the last time I flew anywhere it was in good old economy.

My next video, for 'Stand by Me', was also filmed in LA, but with a different director. What happens is the song is given to different video directors who come back with their ideas on what to do, then the record company chooses one. This time they'd chosen a guy called Wayne Isham, who is another top music video director. He directed Madonna's first video, as well as videos for Led Zeppelin, 'N Sync and Will Smith – this guy was really good.

I met him on the day we arrived because we only had one day to shoot the video. He was directing a video in a graveyard for a rock 'n' roll group when we met, which gave me a feel for what he was like. I didn't know what I'd be doing, but I knew I was in safe hands, so I just went for it. We ended up shooting the video on top of a building with an orchestra and big group of singers; all the women were dressed in black and they are from the best choir in America – R. Kelly has used them and so has P. Diddy. Basically, anyone who's good and needs a choir uses them so it was quite an honour being in such good singing company.

The day we shot the video I saw Bruce Willis. He was staying in the same hotel and just as I was coming out of the lift he walked in. When I got back I told Louis that I'd seen him and said to him, 'You might've been in Die Hard but you'll die easy if you cross me again,' and he said, 'Did you really say that?' Of course I was only winding him up. It was a good one though. Maybe I will next time …

8
THE FAME GAME

I have never wanted to be famous and for that reason I won't change just because I'm a celebrity; I just don't see the point. The day I do is the day I see my career ending, and the day I become a diva is the day people will start talking behind my back. I hope to have a successful career and for people to say I'm a good person. I get more pleasure out of people saying I'm a good singer and a nice guy than anything else. Besides, people can be famous in different ways and I'm famous – God, I even I hate saying that – because I happened to win *X Factor* – that's it. I'm not one of those people that would say, 'Do you know who I am?' That's so pretentious, although not long ago I came very close. I was at the *X Factor: Battle of the Stars* final and had left my drink in the VIP room. The VIP area is only small, but the drinks are free, and there's food if you're hungry, so I went back to get it. A bouncer stopped me and asked to see my wrist band, but I didn't have one. I explained to him that I'd been in there just a minute ago and that all I wanted was my drink, but he wasn't having any of it. I kept thinking, just say who you are, but I couldn't because it would have sounded like I was being a real diva, so in the end I said, 'Look, my name is Shayne Ward, I was in there a second ago, I just want to get my drink and that's it.' He looked a bit embarrassed then and said, 'OK then, you'd better go in!'

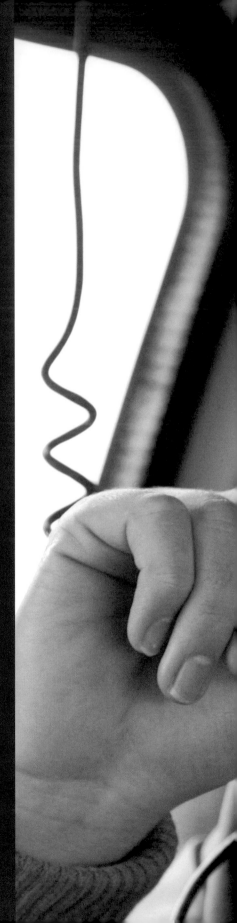

Although my lifestyle has changed drastically and I now have a pad in London, I don't feel famous. I'm still me and I still have the same family, so why should I behave any differently?

All I have ever wanted is to make enough money to help my family get by, but I'm well aware that money can make people miserable, too, and because material things have never been a big part of my life I don't think they ever will be. Of course it's great to have nice stuff, a lovely house or a nice car, but it's not the be all and end all, and if you don't have it you make up for it in other ways. I reckon that not having lots of material stuff made us stronger as a family, and more grateful for everything we have now.

One of the things I really want to do is learn to drive, and not long ago I was offered some free lessons from BSM, so with a bit of luck I'll be on the road soon. The main reason I want to learn to drive is so I can buy myself a nice new car. I think I need something small for London, so maybe a little sporty number or a Mini, but I guess I'd better pass my test first and then decide.

A good friend of mine, Dean, was out filming the documentary for *X Factor*, and they wanted to show where we all were a year ago. I was filmed looking round a BMW showroom. I saw so many nice cars that day that I had to stop myself from buying one, because apart from the fact that I can't actually drive yet, most of the time I'm driven around in nice cars by other people. The paparazzi got a picture of me looking at BMWs that day, which turned up in a couple of newspapers and magazines. I thought it was a bit odd that the photographer knew exactly where we were going to be and what time, but I can't help feeling they probably knew. I'm sure that's the sort of thing people would give one of their dads for.

It's a really weird feeling, too, being able to buy a brand new car, let alone a posh one. When I went to IKEA just the other day looking for furniture, the assistant asked me if I was Shayne Ward. When I said I was, she asked for my autograph and ...

want that, I want that and I want that because I can, I can afford it, I've earned it and I can pay for it.' Whereas before I'd think I'd really like one of them, but I can't buy anything this month. Moments like that really bring home how far I've come. Mind you, I haven't got to the point where I'll splash out on something ridiculous just for the hell of it. I'll only buy what I need – apart from maybe a sports car – and I can't see myself changing the habits of a lifetime. When you've been without, everything is precious.

People feel they have to change to adjust to their new lives in the public eye, but I don't think you have to. I could never click my fingers at people and say, 'Carry this, carry that.' I'm perfectly able to carry my own bags and open my own door. Most of the time now I have a driver and they'll get out and open the door for me, but I always say, 'No, no, don't worry I can do it, but thank you.' I really do think it just comes down to manners and people thinking they have to behave like that because it's expected. I've been really surprised by how quickly people can let that happen. I've seen some people even refuse to sign autographs, which I think is downright stupid. The fans made us and they deserve our time.

I'M PERFECTLY ABLE TO CARRY MY OWN BAGS AND OPEN MY OWN DOOR

When I was a shop assistant in New Look people would often look down their noses at me, but I've always taken great pride in the way I dress and how I look. Louis says that I'll never change, I'll just get better clothes, and now instead of wearing 'Gacci' I'm wearing Gucci! I'd never had a designer name that was real before but the clothes I wear now come from a stylist and I get to keep some of them, which is a real bonus. I do have my say if I don't like what they try and put me in, like skinny jeans – I can't get my head round those at all – I just say thanks, but no thanks. The guy who does *Big Brother's Big Mouth*, Russell Brand, might be able to carry them off, but I'd look like a chicken in them. The most important thing is to be comfortable in what you wear, I reckon.

One magazine feature said I was always wearing the same clothes, but have they never heard of a washing machine? There's no way I'm going to wear something once and never wear it again, that's crazy. I know that some celebrities buy a pair of trainers or a dress, wear it once and that's it, and I guess that's the way they like to be, but I'm not going to be ashamed of wearing something more than once. If you weren't in the limelight no one would ever know. I've got a lot of black jackets, jeans and white shirts that look alike even though they're actually different. I think my stylist took the article to heart, though, as my wardrobe has changed quite a bit since then.

It goes without saying that this business can be pretty cruel and full of shallow people, but I take

that as a lesson of what not to become, and to be honest the worst offenders are usually the Z-listers. One thing I really can't work out is all the women who wear next to nothing. OK it's great on the eye, but leave something to the imagination, ladies, please! Having some of these half-naked women crack on to me is a very weird feeling, mainly because I've never been popular with the ladies. Some girls can be totally shameless and whisper really rude stuff in my ears. Once at an after-show party a girl whispered to me, 'I know you're with your minder, but if you want a bit, follow me in five minutes.' I couldn't believe it – I just laughed because I thought she was joking, but she was deadly serious. Some girls will even follow me and say, 'I know you've got a girlfriend but I'll show you a good time. Come out with me and the girls and we'll get it on.' Honestly, these are exactly the kind of things they say.

When I was being interviewed last Christmas there was an *FHM* shoot with models going on next door and one of them came in wearing next to nothing – she was literally in her bra and pants with her coat open over the top. She passed me a Polaroid of herself with a number on the back and said, 'Call me!' I kept the Polaroid for a bit but when I got home I chucked it away. That wasn't long after I had won *X Factor*, so I was still seriously shockable.

If I'm totally honest no girls ever came near me when I was younger – I've hardly kissed anyone really. My shyness has meant that Fay is only my second serious relationship. I didn't even try it on with girls at school because I knew I'd never get anywhere. Now people tell me that such and such from school likes me and I just think, really? It's not something I'm used to. Don't get me wrong, it's nice, but it's just strange and I think the problem I have now, and the most upsetting thing about it, is that I don't know whether people are genuinely interested in me or just because I've now got a bit of fame; it's hard to know who I can trust and believe. One thing I have learned is that there are a lot of people who are only nice because of the success I've had. When everything kicked off, I had a lot of phone calls from people I hadn't spoken to in ages, like the girls at school who were the 'in' group, the hard lads and the football boys, none of whom would have dreamed of speaking to me before. You have to ask yourself, why now? Would they be talking to me if I hadn't been on TV? And the answer is probably not, so I do have to be careful.

My first serious relationship was with a girl called Natalie Schmitt and we got together when I was about fifteen and in secondary school. We were together for about two years and when I was seventeen we split up. Once I was on *X Factor* it was only a matter of time before she sold her story to the papers. I was in the *X Factor* house and my sister called and said, 'Guess what? Natalie is in the paper with her boobs out doing a kiss-and-tell.' I couldn't believe it – I felt so betrayed. I'm not going to pretend I wasn't gutted, because I was. It was a school romance and I thought that was it. She said a lot of things that weren't true and when I read the article I couldn't believe what she'd done. I just thought, there's your two minutes of fame; I hope it was worth it. There have been other stories and people jumping on the kiss-and-tell bandwagon, and I guess it's an easy way to make money, but I just try to ignore them as, ultimately, I know the truth and so do the important people in my life.

The hardest thing to adapt to since *X Factor* has been the changes in my relationship with Fay; before the show we were together pretty much 24/7 so we're not used to being apart much. All through the competition I was always on the phone to her, telling her how much I missed her and that everything was going great. I have tried to reassure her every step of the way, but as the months passed by and the auditions turned into boot camp, we had very little time together. Even now I don't see her as much as I would like to. I was pre-warned about all this, but it's always harder than you think. I knew that the workload would be enormous and that I wouldn't see much of her, and fortunately she is incredibly supportive and really does understand. I am lucky because I have supportive people all round me and they know that at times being away from my family and Fay can be very hard for me. Fay knows that when I get time off I always spend it with her but she always says, 'Do what you have to do, I will still be here.'

I only get to see her about twice a month if I'm lucky and that's hard on both of us. Sometimes when she comes down she'll stay with my auntie, just on the off chance I can get some time off to see her, but it's often a wasted journey. Once I was chosen as Louis' final four and the shows began, Fay would come down every week to watch me perform on the Saturday show – I think people thought we spent quite a lot of time together, but in fact we didn't as there was only time to sneak a kiss at the end of the night. Trying to spread my time was a nightmare and Fay didn't come back with me to the house once, there simply wasn't time. Every day we'd have rehearsals and our schedules were so tight there was only time to practise our songs for the following week.

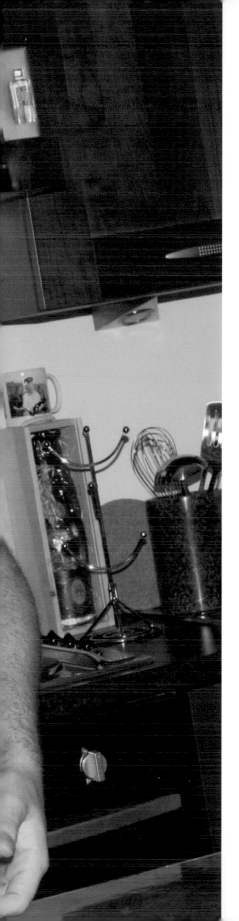

The upside is that absence really does make the heart grow fonder. The more I'm away from Fay the more I miss her, and the same goes for the rest of my family. Don't get me wrong, I would love to see her all the time, but this is a good test and I think our relationship can stand it. People forget what a strong bond we have because we've been together so long, and I'm very lucky that Fay is happy to let my career take the front seat for the time being. Who knows what the future will bring, but at this moment in time Fay and I are happy. One of the questions I am asked most often is whether Fay is jealous and I can honestly say she isn't. She knows that I'm not going to be stupid and jeopardise what I have with her; I would never do anything daft like that and I hope that we can stand the test of time. I would just like to point out, though, just because I have a girlfriend it doesn't stop me loving all the attention I get, and she knows that, but we trust each other and she knows it would never go any further.

The way I see it, you can enjoy temptation without giving in to it, and to be honest I think I still wouldn't even if I was single. Things happen and people make mistakes, but it's never long before they realise what they've lost. Even if I was single I wouldn't sleep my way through a bunch of girls; it's not me and it's not the way I behave. I'm sure a lot of twenty-two-year-old blokes think I'm mad but I want to focus on my career. I'm not a big showbiz person and the whole idea of it doesn't feel comfortable to me. I go to clubs but I'm not a clubber, I would rather go to a local bar with my family and friends to have a drink. I don't want to throw my career away because of stupid mistakes, and I want a long career, not just success that lasts a week or two.

The showbiz world can be a cruel place and I don't want Fay to get mixed up in it. I think some people who become showbiz couples lose sight of what they became famous for. Doing a shoot with Fay for a magazine is not a road I want to go down

at this moment in time; it would feel as though I was selling out somehow, and turning up week in week out in the same magazine doesn't appeal to me. If you're everywhere people get sick of you, and I'd rather not let that happen. Louis once said to me, 'Shayne, have you ever seen Tom Jones's wife?' I knew exactly what he meant by that. I haven't ever seen her, but I know that she has stood by him throughout his career, without being in the public eye, and he's enjoyed both an amazing career and a long, happy marriage.

I remember just after I'd won some guy came up to me and said, 'You need to upgrade now; you need to find a model for a girlfriend.' I thought that was a really horrible comment to make and it made me realise what sort of business I was getting into. I just turned round to him and said, 'Fay knows that my music is my focus at the moment and is behind me 100 per cent. She knows that she has nothing to worry about. I won't jeopardise what I have with her.'

I know the papers are waiting for me to break up with her and say that the only reason I haven't done it sooner is because it would have looked bad on me, but they'll just have to carry on waiting because it won't happen. Even if we did split up we would still be friends, but right now we are both passionate about each other. I love her and I can't imagine my life without her. Marriage, children and even engagement are a very long way off, though, because while I love Fay very much, it's the music first at the moment. And the same goes for her as her career is beginning to take off, too, with a part in the *Hollyoaks* spin-off.

I guess one of the biggest changes in my life has been the circles I mix in and the celebrities I get to meet, like Robbie Williams. It's the kind of things I could only dream of before, and now suddenly it's become a reality.

When I won *X Factor* I shook Louis' hands and promised him I would never change – I'm a man of my word and I won't. I'm sure loads of people say that when they set out on the road to fame, but I really mean it. I don't want to be somebody I'm not and it's for that reason that I won't jeopardise what I have with Fay. Louis has had great faith in me and I don't want to let him down – I want to make him proud.

Earlier this year Louis and Ashley took me to David and Victoria Beckham's World Cup party, which was a real experience. James Brown was playing, and when he started to sing I was straight up on the dance floor busting some moves. Wayne Rooney was there and everyone was worried he wouldn't be fit for the World Cup because of his foot injury. When Wayne walked in I went over and said hi to his girlfriend, Colleen, saying, 'We have something in common.' She said, 'What's that?' And I said, 'We both used to work in New Look.' At that point Wayne, who was standing next to her, said, 'So what's going on here, lads,' and that's how we got chatting. We talked about *X Factor* and I wished him luck with the World Cup and his foot – I knew his injury couldn't have been too bad because before long he and I were having dance competitions. The whole country panicking about whether or not he'd be able to play and I was dancing with him at the Beckhams' house – now that was surreal.

The party was a proper star-studded bash and there were loads of big names wandering about – I couldn't believe how many of them recognised me. Even David Beckham's mum came up to me and whispered, 'I voted for you!' I don't know why, but I took her hand, kissed it and said thank you very much.

As the evening wore on I started to relax a bit and be less nervous so when I saw Gordon Ramsey I went up and said hello. I think people find him intimidating, but he was really nice to me. While Gordon and I were chatting about the party, his show The F Word and his projects in America, a lady came over and joined us, and I have to say she was really boring. Conversation was drying up and we were dying to get away, so I decided to try my fool-proof trick: I pretended to answer my phone. Obviously no one was there, but she didn't know that so it was the perfect reason for me to excuse myself. A couple of seconds later I said, 'Er, Gordon, it's for you' and I think he realised what I'd done because he took the call and the woman left. He was so grateful and we laughed our heads off. That particular trick has helped me out in a lot of situations.

Everyone seemed to want to ask me about *X Factor* and what it felt like to win the show and they were all congratulating me – I was so surprised to find out that so many people had watched.

Being a massive football fan, it was also great to see loads of players' faces. Liverpool's Steven Gerrard, who I really rate as a footballer, was there and he came over and congratulated me, too, which I thought was great of him.

The one thing I couldn't believe was how small David Beckham is. A lot of celebrities are much smaller than you think when you meet them, and he is definitely one of them.

I THINK
I'M ON THE
WAY TO
MAKING IT

Ashley introduced me to him but I only spoke to him for a couple of minutes as it was his party and everyone wanted time with him, but he congratulated me and introduced me to Victoria. At the end of the night just as I was about to leave, David came over to say goodbye. He said, 'Well done again, mate, congratulations and good luck in your career.' I said thank you and I thanked him for the invite. It was an incredible night and I felt privileged to be there and to have met so many interesting people.

Another great star-studded do I went to was Elton John's White Tie and Tiara ball and it was fantastic. It was held at Elton's house in a big marquee in his garden and I went along with Simon and Louis. It was amazing to see Take That and Elton perform and to be invited to such a great party – it was mad. There was an Indian theme and everything looked really spectacular – the money and effort that goes into a party like that must be enormous. Even when we were sitting down eating our dinner I spent the whole time looking round the room, staring at faces I've only ever seen on TV or in magazines. I still can't quite believe I was there.

I was tripping over famous people at Elton's party so it was pretty strange, having met lots of them in the flesh, to then go to Madame Tussaud's and see them all again. Being the first reality TV star to make it into the wax museum was quite something. At first I worried that it was too soon and that people would criticise me for it, but then I just thought, who cares? It's an honour and I'm in there because the public want to see me there. I only had to go for one casting, then they took some photographs of me and a load of measurements and within weeks it was on display. I went to open it and couldn't believe how realistic it was. When Mum saw it I think she wanted to take it home. To me Madame Tussaud's is like the hallowed hall of fame and seeing myself there was the first time I thought, do you know what, I think I'm on the way to making it. Seriously,

though, I don't think I'll ever feel like I've made it

These days I really can't go anywhere without being recognised – even if I just go to the shop I get attention. Sometimes when people come up to me and say, 'Hi, Shayne', at first I try and pretend it's not me, but they never believe me and I always end up giving them my autograph. If I wear a cap I can go unnoticed for a little longer, like say maybe five minutes, but that's about it. Weirdly, and I never thought I'd say this, I do miss reality and normality but I know that this could be it for me, potentially, for ever, and I wouldn't really have it any other way – it's a small price to pay for what I have in return.

It's also hard to get my head round how popular I've become in other countries. I did an interview in Korea not long ago, where they were going mad over me, and they wanted to know when I was doing an international tour. The girl interviewing me asked if I knew a football player called Song who plays for Manchester United and I went, 'Yeah I know Song the footballer. I've seen him play.' 'Oh my God, Shayne knows Song!' she said. She couldn't believe it, everything was Oh my God this, Oh my God that – she was so excited it was hilarious.

When I look back on it, the amount of things I've done in the last ten months are more than I could have hope for, like my first-class aeroplane trip or travelling by helicopter. That was really something, the helicopter ride. After a surprise gig for the auditionees for *X Factor* 2006 at Old Trafford in Manchester, I had to get to my next appearance. My schedule was so tight I had to leave almost straight after singing to perform in Weston-super-Mare at T4 on the Beach. I couldn't believe how quickly we got there. We drove straight over to the concert venue and all the way up to the stage, where I was taken backstage to get ready. As I walked through the marquee people were asking me for my autograph and shouting my name – the crowd was amazing. I haven't had a bad reception yet and I hope never to experience one. When I walked out on stage I couldn't believe how many banners had my name on them – I don't think that will ever stop shocking me – and I'll always be grateful to my amazing fans as they seemed to know every word of my songs and were all singing along with me.

After the performance I did some interviews backstage. If you walked along the beach you could see where the interviews were being done and it wasn't long before people cottoned on and started to come round screaming. The poor interviewer had a bit of job hearing over the noise. All I did was lift a finger and they would go completely mad – it's reassuring to know that a good few months on, the fans are still there. Thank you to them.

People think I'm already a millionaire, but trust me, I'm not. I have a million-pound record contract, but that doesn't mean I'm going to get a million pounds in my bank account. Out of that contract everyone needs to get paid – photographers, make-up artists, stylists, security, PR people, accommodation, travel. Everything costs money. For me to earn money I need to do personal

PEOPLE THINK I'M ALREADY A MILLIONAIRE, BUT TRUST ME, I'M NOT

appearances, private parties and things like that, and the sales of the album and singles help, too, of course. I did the Woolworths advert last Christmas and it's things like that that pay the bills.

Not long ago I sang at number 11 Downing Street for a party Gordon Brown was having to celebrate the launch of a newspaper for kids. I did an acoustic session and I sang 'That's My Goal' and 'No Promises'. Each experience is different and great in its own way, but that was a weird one – I was in the house next to our Prime Minister for a start! The house is huge, with big Victorian rooms, and I couldn't believe the period detail everywhere and the number of books and old paintings. They were a great audience, and afterwards they were very complimentary and really seemed to enjoy the songs, which I was relieved about because I didn't want to upset Mr Brown. Just before I left, Gordon thanked me and passed me a box of chocolates. He told me he had read somewhere that I never got any freebies, so he gave me a box of House of Commons' Victorian mints which I keep in my fridge and still haven't opened. They're a nice reminder of the day ... every time I open the door for the milk!

9

THE FUTURE
IS BRIGHT

Both my life and my family's lives have changed dramatically and are unlikely to go back to the way they were ever again. Even my mum gets stopped in the street to sign autographs and I sometimes feel bad that she can't go out for a coffee without being noticed, but she doesn't complain; she's taken it all in her stride. Signing autographs and answering questions is just part of being in the public eye and people in Clayton and Manchester got so behind me during *X Factor* a few autographs doesn't seem a lot to ask for. I think all of my brothers' and sisters' lives have changed a bit since I won but they all carry on with their everyday jobs; they just get recognised sometimes, too. Emma and Leona both work in the shopping centre and Lisa works for a catering company. Not one of them would think, oh, our Shayne is doing well for himself, so I think I'll stop work now; they have more respect than that.

Each one of us has been offered a lot of money to sell our stories – even Mum – but we are pretty private and such a close family. Even here, I've found it hard to open up and I find talking about personal issues very difficult, but I've been as full and frank about things as I can and I hope that has come across. I've always found it hard to let people in, especially where my family relationships are concerned.

I'm slowly trying to juggle my new life with seeing Fay and my family, but it's not easy – for a start we all live in different towns. Everything is different now and my life is in London, although I think wherever you were brought up is where you call home, and someday I will definitely go back. However, unless they open a Sony BMG office in Manchester, or Louis and Ashley open an office there, there just isn't any work for me; it's all in London. For the moment I'm just enjoying this ride and living each exciting day to the full.

I speak to my family and Fay as often as I can; I usually spend a couple of hours calling round everyone because it's a lot easier. I've got a lot of brothers and sisters, my mum and Fay to call, and if I missed anyone out I would be in big trouble. It's always good to hear their voices, especially when I get lonely.

My mum came to see my flat for the first time about a month ago. I wanted to get it all sorted and kitted out before she came to visit, so I could make her really proud of what I've done to the place. I've bought most of my stuff from IKEA because it's a really modern minimalist apartment – in fact, the only thing I spent a lot of money on was a massive plasma TV, which sits in the corner

I'VE ALWAYS FOUND IT
HARD TO LET PEOPLE IN,
ESPECIALLY WHERE MY
FAMILY RELATIONSHIPS
ARE CONCERNED

of my sitting room. I've also got a few professional pictures of me up in the flat because I had a shoot done by a guy called Neil Kirk and I liked them so much I had a couple blown up. I first had the idea when I saw one of Alicia Keys' pictures in the hallway of Sony BMG – but I'm not vain, though, honest.

Winning *X Factor* has given me such joy because it's made my mum so proud. Can you tell I'm a real mummy's boy?! I can't fully explain how I feel, and I don't expect people to understand, but I would die for my mum – anything she wants I'd try to get for her. If something was wrong with her and I had to end my career tomorrow, that's exactly what I'd do. I even have a nickname for her – Blue Eyes, like Frank Sinatra – because she has beautiful piercing blue eyes that are lighter than the sky. Every time I phone her I sing Elton John's 'Blue Eyes' to her and it makes her laugh. We all love her dearly.

One thing I really must sort out is the holiday I promised my mum. I keep nagging her to get a passport, but she seems a bit reluctant and I think she might be afraid of flying. I'm determined that she's going to go, though, even if I have to sort it all out myself. I can't believe that she's never been abroad and I'd love her to experience the feeling of getting off a plane in another country – I know that once she gets there she'll really enjoy it. When we were younger she could never afford to take us further than Blackpool, so to go away now would be a real treat for her.

I'm so happy that my mum has now found someone who treats her well and who loves her. She and Phil have been together for about two years now and he is her first serious boyfriend since she and Dad split up. Early on she met someone else who didn't work out – it was kind of a rebound thing. I'm very protective of Mum, and when she does get together with someone new it always feels a bit weird, but Phil is the only person who has stood out and really put a smile on her face.

I KNOW THE MUSIC BUSINESS IS A FICKLE INDUSTRY

My mum's full name is Philomena, Mena for short, but now she's with Phil we make fun of them and call them Phil and Mena. Mum deserves some happiness, and I think with Phil she's really found that. He treats her really well and I always hear him telling her how much he loves her. They don't live together, but I'm sure that once my sisters have moved out he will move in. My little sister Leona is eighteen now, so it won't be long before she gets her own place. The bottom line is that if my mum's happy, we are happy. Phil has a family from a previous marriage and they live in Ireland, so if they do get married, which I hope they will, we'll be one very big Irish family.

I know the music business is a fickle industry, and that I need to be sensible with the money I make. Our family has always struggled, so I want to set myself up as best I can for the future so I can look after everyone. It's great to be able to help Mum financially so she doesn't have to work any more – all the worrying is down to me now, which I prefer.

I'm investing all the money I make and I'd like to invest it in houses. Obviously I hope my career will go from strength to strength and that I won't have to worry about things like that, but I don't want to take any risks. If I can afford it I would like to buy another little flat and rent it out, so I can make money that way as well. Shane from Westlife has done this and I think property is the way to go when it comes to investing. If things

continue to go well for me and I end up working and earning good money, I told my brother Michael that I'll make him a landlord. I'll buy him a small apartment and rent it out, but I'll hand him the keys and put his name on the deeds so he's the landlord. He couldn't believe it when I told him, but I mean it. I'll do it if I can because he deserves a break in life, and if I can be the one to give it to him, then I will.

I have so many ambitions and plans but one thing I'd really like to try my hand at is acting, like Will Young. I haven't done any since I was at school but I'd love to give it a go and see if I'm any good – Fay thinks I would be. If I could choose I'd like a part in *Shameless* because that show is brilliant, or maybe a horror movie, because they're my favourite kind, providing I got to be the hero. I'd be really flattered to be asked to audition for something.

Although I never thought I would be famous I have let my imagination run wild a few times and thought about who I would like to manage me – weirdly enough, I always wanted to be managed by Louis Walsh and signed to Simon's record label, so now that I am it's like all my dreams have come true. Work doesn't stop though and my next big project is going international, but I've only had a short stint abroad to find out what other countries think of my music. I've been to Australia, Asia, Hong Kong, South Africa and various other countries and the response has been very positive so I hope to be returning soon, but now it's not long before I start my debut UK tour.

I am so excited about seeing my fans again in 2007 and I feel really proud to be appearing at such big venues. Being on the road is the one time you can get close to your fans and it's been a while since I performed for them. I know that a lot of people would like to see me do some more up-tempo tunes and a bit of dancing on stage, like when I sang Justin Timberlake's song on *X Factor*, so I'm going to do something really special for the shows. I did a lot of dancing at school – there's even a picture of me dressed up as Elvis in here somewhere – and I'm busy getting fit for the tour so I can perform my best on stage; I've even joined a gym and got myself a personal trainer.

Another ambition I have is to crack America, but I want to establish myself here in the UK 100 per cent first. This is where I started and this is where my fan base is – I'll only go to America if I have the backing of the UK and Ireland. If you go and you don't make it, you need to be sure your fans back home will still be waiting for you, and you can only guarantee that if you spend time here and treat them with the respect they deserve.

All of my ambitions are dependent on one thing – my voice – and since that amazing night in G-A-Y I've been struggling with the tear in one of my vocal cords. The crunch came when I was recently in LA and I had a career make-or-break decision to take.

I was recording some of my new tracks for the second album and was talking to one of the guys in the studio about the problem I was having with my nodule. He suggested going to see a specialist

called Doctor Kantor and told me that he was the best doctor around when it came to throats. As soon as I'd made an appointment and walked into his waiting room I knew he had to be pretty good; the walls were lined with photos of famous singers like Mariah Carey, Michael Jackson, Meatloaf and Michael Bolton. He had treated them all successfully so that made me feel a little bit more relaxed about everything.

After examining my throat, Dr Kantor told me that I needed to have surgery on the nodule to have it removed. This scared me so much but I knew in my heart of hearts that I needed to have it done and that if anyone was going to do it then this was the right specialist. After the consultation I phoned everyone – Mum, Louis, Simon and Sonny – to ask for their advice. They all said they would be behind my decision 100% and didn't at any point push me into having the op. With every kind of surgery there are risks and I was really aware of them. I knew that it could be the end but I made the decision to do it: to have the surgery to save my voice.

I had the operation on the 31 August 2006. It was a terrifying prospect and I had been psyching myself up for days. I sat in the waiting room with all the worst scenarios running through my mind before eventually being called in. I was given a general anaesthetic and as I was being wheeled into the operating theatre I said to the doctor; 'That's what I do, I sing and I want my voice back.' It's the last thing I remember before waking up in the recovery room.

When I went back to the hotel I wasn't allowed to speak for six days – not a word. Let me tell you, it's more difficult than it sounds and by Day 6 I was beginning to get really frustrated. I walked around with a pad and a pen and wrote down everything: I'd be in the bar and want a drink so I would have to write 'lemonade please' and show the barman. It did have its benefits though – when I went and bought two DVDs the shop keeper put a free one in the bag – I think he felt sorry for me!

On the seventh day I went back to see Dr Kantor and he showed me the before and after x-ray and he was really pleased with the results. Even I could see what a good job had been done and I was over the moon, I was so relieved.

When I first started speaking again my voice was very croaky and I communicated with Faye in a kind of noise language: one sniff for yes and two for no. When I began to talk she could barely understand me but since then my voice has grown stronger and stronger. And I have just started singing again – half an hour each day – and thankfully I can hit those high notes. Although I will have to have regular check-ups with my local GP, the worst is over.

I have started recording bits and pieces and the music I am working on for the new album is far more up-beat and up-tempo than before. I hope I'll get to duet with other artists in the near future too as it would add a really interesting dimension to the new material. It's an exciting time as the album is shaping up to be completely different to my last and there'll be a single release before the end of the year as a taster ... so watch this space!

I truly believe my future is bright. I've been given such an opportunity by winning *X Factor* and I hope to make the most of it. This last year has been a rollercoaster ride: I've gone from working at New Look, to auditioning in front of Louis, Sharon and Simon, surviving boot camp and performing on live TV in front of millions to releasing my own single and album – and what I've learned is to take every experience as it comes. From my childhood and the struggles we had, I know that what matters is family, friends and relationships, and anything worth having is worth working for. I'm a pretty shy person, but one thing I'm not shy of is hard work and I will do everything to be here as long as I can and sing my heart out and in the process, I hope, entertain.

My album was a big success, and I've got one number one under my belt, but I want to achieve more. I can't wait to share the new material with my fans. I hope they like it; it is definitely from the heart.

I will be forever grateful to my fans, and to everyone who has supported me through this amazing time. Without you, I'd be nothing.

So, I guess you could say this is the beginning of my story. I'm here to stay and I'll give everything I have to live this dream.

ACKNOWLEDGEMENTS

I would like to thank my managers Louis Walsh and Ashley Tabor for guiding me so wisely and making everything possible. To Dan Parker who has worked so hard to make sure this project is successful. I would also like to say a big thank you to Hannah Perry who made the whole process of writing this book a lot of fun, and Amanda Harris and all at Orion for their hard work.

PICTURE CREDITS

From Shayne's own family album
p. 18, p. 21, p. 40, p. 42.
Caroline Cooper
p. 6–7, p. 8–9, p. 12, p. 20, p. 23, p. 27, p. 31, p. 35, p. 36–37, p. 39, p. 41, p. 44, p. 47, p. 51, p. 52–53, p. 56–57, p. 59, p. 60, p. 62, p. 65, p. 66, p. 69, p. 70, p. 75, p. 78, p. 79, p. 80, p. 83, p. 86, p. 88–89, p. 90, p. 91, p. 92–93, p. 94–95, p. 96, p. 97, p. 99, p. 100–101, p. 104–105, p. 110–111, p. 112–113, p. 116–117, p. 119, p. 122–123, p. 128, p. 130, p. 132–133, p. 135, p. 136, p. 138–139, p. 141, p. 143, p. 144, p. 148–149, p. 152–153, p. 154–155, p. 157, p. 158, p. 159, p. 160, p. 164, p. 166, p. 169, p. 171, p. 172, p. 175, p. 176–177, p. 179, p. 184.
Patricia McMahon
p. 2–3, p. 14–15, p. 17, p. 24, p. 54, p. 72–73, p. 102, p. 107, p. 120, p. 147, p. 150, p. 162, p. 180–181, p. 188–189.
Ellis Parrinder
p. 5, p. 32, p. 48, p. 64, p. 84–85, p. 114, p. 126, p. 182–183, p. 186–187.